GROVER CLEVELAND
1837 — 1908

Chronology—Documents—Bibliographical Aids

Edited by
ROBERT I. VEXLER

Series Editor
HOWARD F. BREMER

Oceana Publications, Inc.
Dobbs Ferry, N.Y.
1968

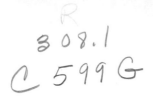

© Copyright 1968 by Oceana Publications, Inc.

Library of Congress Catalog Card Number 68-21538
Oceana Book No. 303-4

Printed in the United States of America

CONTENTS

BIBLIOGRAPHICAL AIDS

EDITOR'S FOREWORD

Every attempt has been made to cite the most accurate dates in this Chronology. Diaries, documents, letters, and similar evidence have been used to determine the exact date. If, however, later scholarship has found such dates to be obviously erroneous, the more plausible date has been used. Should this Chronology be in conflict with other authorities, the student is urged to go back to original sources as well as to such careful biographers as Allan Nevins.

This is a research tool compiled primarily for the student. While it does make some judgments on the significance of the events, it is hoped that they are reasoned judgments based on a long acquaintance with American History.

Obviously, the very selection of events by any writer is itself a judgment.

The essence of these little books is in their making available some pertinent facts and key documents **plus** a critical bibliography which should direct the student to investigate for himself additional and/or contradictory material. The works cited may not always be available in small libraries, but neither are they usually the old, out of print, type of book often included in similar accounts. Documents in this volume are taken from James D. Richardson, ed., **Messages and Papers of the Presidents.** Vols. 7 and 8, 1913 edition.

CHRONOLOGY

1837
March 18   Born, Caldwell, New Jersey. Father: Richard Cleveland. Mother: Ann Neal.

1841
Family moved to Fayetteville, New York.

1846
Rose Cleveland born. She was to be mistress of the White House for her bachelor brother.

1850
Fall   Visited his Uncle Lewis F. Allen at Black Rock just outside Buffalo, New York.

Family moved to Clinton, New York. Father became District Secretary of the Central New York Agency of the American Home Missionary Society.

Winter   Attended Clinton Liberal Institute.

1852
Spring   Returned to Fayetteville to be a clerk in the store of Deacon John McVicar.

1853
February 3   Along with other students at Fayetteville Academy organized a debating society or "gymnasium." Elected Vice Archon.

September   Family moved to Holland Patent, New York near Utica.

October 1   Father, Richard died.

October 5   Appointed Assistant teacher at the New York Institution for the Blind. Brother William appointed Principal Male Teacher.

1854
Fall   Left New York.

Winter	Back in Holland Patent. Read Latin some evenings.

1855

Spring	Left Holland Patent with another boy for Ohio.
May 21	Visited Uncle Lewis F. Allen who persuaded him to stay in Buffalo.
August	Appointed clerk and copyist for a Buffalo, New York law firm of Rogers, Bowen and Rogers at no salary. Then given a salary of $4.00 per week. In 1858 his salary was raised to $500 per year. Left firm beginning of 1863.

1859

May	Admitted to the Bar.

1861

Helped edit a book about cattle.

1862

October 30	Nominated for Ward Supervisor. Elected to post in November.

1863

Assistant District Attorney of Erie County, New York, for a two year term.

July	Cleveland's name was one of first drawn in Buffalo under the Conscription Act of March 3, 1863. He could not go because of the need to support his family. Paid $150 to a substitute.

1865

Nominated for District Attorney. Defeated in November election by Republican opponent, Lyman K. Bass.

1866

Became partner of former State Treasurer Isaac K. Vanderpoel in a law firm.

1868

September	Delegate to the Democratic State Convention in Albany.

1870

September 26	Nominated for Sheriff of Erie County. Elected in November elections.

1871

January 1	Took office as Sheriff of Erie County for a two year term.

1872

September 6 Superintended the hanging of Patrick Morissey, who was convicted of stabbing his mother. Cleveland refused to hire an agent to do this task.

1873

February 14 Took charge of hanging of Jack Gaffney, a gambler, convicted of shooting and killing a man in a card game at Buffalo.

1874—1881

Formed law partnership with Lyman K. Bass and Wilson S. Bissell.

1877

Helped found the City Club in Buffalo. Was one of the original members of the board of directors.

1881

October 25 Nominated for Mayor of Buffalo. Elected to the post in November.

1882

January 1 Took oath of office as Mayor of Buffalo. Made successful attacks against graft and corruption. Because of his veto of many bills became known as "veto mayor."

June 26 Veto of Street Cleaning contract which was outright graft charging $50,000 more than was necessary.

July 3 Spoke at Semi-Centennial Celebration of the City of Buffalo.

July 19 Mother, Ann died.

August 23 Edgar K. Apgar wrote to Cleveland urging him to be a candidate for the Democratic nomination for Governor of New York State.

September 20 Republican State Convention refused to nominate Governor Alonzo Cornell for another term. Named Secretary of the Treasury Charles J. Folger.

September 21 Democratic State Convention opened at Syracuse.

September 22 Nominated for Governor.

October 28   Wrote letter to New York Civil Service Reform Association stating that he approved of the principles involved in the Pendleton bill relating to civil service reform.

November 7   Cleveland elected Governor of New York State.

December 5   Delivered speech at the Manhattan Club in New York.

1883

January 1   Inaugurated as Governor of New York State.

March 2   Vetoed Five Cent Fare bill: a measure to reduce the fare on the New York City Elevated Railroad from ten to five cents. In his uncompromising defense of the letter of the law Cleveland maintained that this was against the Charter of the company. Would work for revision of charter to have fare reduced.

April 9   Vetoed amendments to the Charter of Buffalo.

May 4   Indicated in a message to the New York Senate that he had nominated a worthy individual for the post of Immigration Commissioner, whom the Senate was refusing to confirm.

June 1   Signed the New York City Aqueduct Bill.

November 2   Wrote a letter to Mr. Kelly of Tammany Hall requesting Senator Grady's retirement.

1884

Vetoed the Maximum Hours Law for conductors and drivers of horse-drawn streetcars who were working 14-16 hours per day. The Bill had been so amended that although it limited the workday to 10 hours, it permitted longer hours of work for extra compensation.

January 8   Presided over New York State Bar Association at Albany.

March 17   Signed three bills introduced by Theodore Roosevelt reorganizing the governments of New York City and New York County.

June 3-6   Republican National Convention at Chicago, Illinois, nominated James Gillespie Blaine of Maine for President, and John Alexander Logan of Illinois for Vice-President.

June 8   Carl Schurz bolted the Republican Party because of Blaine's nomination which he did not approve.

June 30   Wrote to Daniel Manning, a prominent New York Democrat, in regard to the nomination possibilities that he was willing to remain Governor of New York State, but would accept nomination for President.

July 8-11   Democratic National Convention at Chicago, Illinois, nominated Grover Cleveland for President, and Thomas Andrew Hendricks of Indiana for Vice-President.

July 21   Republicans began a public assault on Cleveland for a private life scandal. He was supposedly the father of the illegitimate child of Maria Halpin.

September 12   Endorsed by Tammany Hall organization.

October 29   A delegation of Protestant clergymen met in New York. Dr. Samuel Burchard referred to the Democrats as the party of "rum, Romanism, and rebellion." This insult to the Catholic Church and the Democratic Party hurt the Republicans. They failed to carry New York State by 1200 votes.

Blaine attended a dinner tendered by Jay Gould and Russell Sage which won him more notoriety because of his connection with these "money kings."

November 4   Election day. The election remained in doubt for three days. Then Cleveland was recognized as elected. Cleveland received a total of 4,875,971 votes, winning 219 electoral votes. Blaine received 4,852,234 votes, winning 182 electoral votes.

December 25   Addressed public letter to George William Curtis, President of the National Civil Reform League. Announced that he would adhere strictly to the Civil Service Reform Law of 1883, applying its principles to the large class of employees not within the law. Only inefficient and unscrupulous individuals would be removed before their term of office was up.

1885

January 23   The Germans seized Samoan territory.

February 4-7   Visited New York for conferences on Cabinet posts.

February 28   Signed a letter addressed to Representative A. J. Warner and other members of the 48th Congress in which he defied the silver men by indicating that he would use gold as well as silver coinage.

FIRST TERM IN OFFICE

1885

March 4   Inaugurated. Oath administered by Chief Justice Morrison Remick Waite.

March 6   Cabinet Officers appointed: Secretary of State Thomas Francis Bayard of Delaware, Secretary of the Treasury Daniel Manning of New York (entered upon duties March 8), Secretary of War William Crowinshield Endicott of Massachusetts, Attorney General Augustus Hill Garland (entered upon duties March 9), Postmaster General William Freeman Vilas of Wisconsin, Secretary of the Navy William Collins Whitney of New York, and Secretary of the Interior Lucius Quintus Cincinnatus Lamar of Mississippi.

March   In order to counteract the threat to the gold reserve, Cleveland and Manning adopted rigorous measures, discontinuing President Arthur's policy allowing Federal revenues to accumulate in the vault.

March 13   Withdrew certain treaties pending in the Senate: commercial treaties between the United States and the Dominican Republic and Spain; and a treaty between the United States and Nicaragua for building an interoceanic canal.

March 29   Abram S. Hewitt turned down offer of Ministership to Russia, Spain, or Austria in order to remain a Democratic leader in the House of Representatives.

April   Commissioner Sparks of the Land Office issued a sweeping order suspending all action in the General Land Office upon entries in most of the trans-Mississippi West except private cash entries and certain landscrip locations to permit investigation of fraudulent claims.

April 2   Withdrew Treaty of Friendship, Commerce and Navigation concluded between the United States and the Argentine Confederation which had been communicated to the Senate, January 27, 1885.

April 17   Issued Proclamation declaring inoperative President Arthur's order of February 27, throwing the Old Winnebago and Crow Creek Reservations in the Dakota Territory open to the public domain. Gave 60 days notice to vacate the land.

May 17   Apache Chief Geronimo on warpath in Arizona and New Mexico. After having the uprising suppressed Cleveland pressed for legislation in regard to land ownership and citizenship for Indians.

July 23   Ulysses S. Grant died. Cleveland attended the funeral in New York and then went to the Adirondacks for a vacation.

Cleveland gave "40 Days Notice" to cattlemen who were encroaching upon Indian Reservations in the Southwest. They had to drive their stock out of the area within the allotted time. This order was received with vigorous protest by Eastern investors and Western cattlemen because of the inadequate notice.

August 7   Issued Proclamation striking at ranchers who were fencing in government lands and water courses. Denounced these enclosures and called upon Federal officers to demolish them.

September 3   Naval War College opened at Newport, Rhode Island.

September 11   Formally recognized the Independent State of the Congo.

Accepted Dorman B. Eaton's resignation as member of the Board of Civil Service Commissioners. Took this opportunity to indicate how much he believed in civil-service reform.

October 27   Statement to public that after November 1 the President will not grant interviews to those seeking public positions or their advocates.

November 25   Vice-President Thomas Hendricks died.

November 27	Approved rules confirming and extending the civil service regulations.

1886

January 19	Presidential Succession Act approved, providing for the succession to the Presidency of the heads of the executive departments in order of the creation of their offices in the event of the death, resignation, or removal of both the President and Vice-President.
February 7	Anti-Chinese riots in Washington Territory.
February 8	Signed the Dawes Act or "Indian Emancipation Act" which made possible the disestablishment of the reservation system and the transforming of the Indians from wards of the government into men in a world of men.
March 1	Made a formal appeal to the country concerning the rights of the President in regard to the suspension or removal of officials.
March 6	Shopmen struck against the Texas and Pacific Railroad which was under a receivership. The strike spread to other railroads.
March 10	Sent to Congress the first of his pension bills.
March 26	Governors at Missouri, Kansas, Arkansas, and Texas issued proclamations calling on managers to send out their trains as usual. Law officers were to give them protection.
March 29	Washington and New York papers announced on authority of several Republican Senators that there would be few if any further calls for information on appointments.
April 22	Because of strikes of 1886, issued the first message to Congress upon the subject of labor in American History. Urged that the workers be given greater benefits and rights.
May 4	Haymarket Riot in Chicago in which a bomb was thrown by anarchists, killing seven and harming the labor movement.
	Strike against railroads was terminated.

May 7	Fisheries' trouble with Canada began. Canadians seized the schooner **David J. Adams.**
May 8	Special veto of pension bills, complaining of so many bills using the principle that the Pensions Bureau was fully capable of judging fairly in all cases. Congress was setting itself up as a rival pensions court.
May 11	Recommended to Congress that it appropriate the necessary funds for the dedication of the Statue of Liberty.
May 17	Act passed providing for commissioning of graduates of United States Military Academy as second lieutenants.
May 25	Announcement of President's plans to marry Frances Folsom.
June 1	Requested Secretary Manning, who was ill, to take a leave of absence until October 1 and then decide whether to resign or not.
June 2	Married to Frances Folsom, his ward, who was 21 and had just graduated from Wells College. Only President married in the White House. Mrs. Cleveland added a great deal to the social life of Washington. The Marine Band under the directorship of John Philip Sousa played at the wedding.
June	The Tenure of Office Act of 1867, which was modified in 1869, was completely repealed thus removing restrictions upon the President in regard to suspensions and removal of officials.
June 17	House of Representatives refused to consider the Morrison Tariff bill, 157-140.
July 14	Issued a letter warning officeholders not to use their positions to control local politics.
Mid July	Visited upstate New York.
August 2	Signed bill placing a tax upon oleomargarine, suggesting certain amendments.
August 20	Chicago anarchists convicted of murder.

October 21   Visited Richmond, Virginia and State Fair Grounds.

October 28   Dedication of Statue of Liberty.

November 8   Speech at Harvard University's 250th Anniversary. Discussed dignity of the Presidency and relationships with the press.

November 14   Visited Boston.

November 16   Wrote to M. E. Benton stating that he would rescind order suspending him because he proved that his speaking engagements had not interfered with his official work.

November 18   Ex-President Chester Arthur died. Funeral November 22.

November 23   Wrote to Attorney General Garland discussing the suspension of Federal District Attorney William A. Stone of Pennsylvania, a Republican, for having participated in political activities. Stone was not reinstated because he had betrayed the trust placed upon him by the administration by supporting Republicans for office.

December 8   American Federation of Labor organized. Samuel Gompers, first president.

1887

January 14   Senate passed Interstate Commerce bill.

January 21   The House of Representatives passed the Interstate Commerce bill.

February 4   Interstate Commerce Act approved. The Act was passed as a result of discriminatory railroad practices and applied to railroads passing through more than one state. The Interstate Commerce Commission, the first regulatory commission in the United States history was established.

February 11   Vetoed the Blair Dependent Pension bill for special pensions. Under this bill any man who had served 90 days in the army during any war need only claim that he could not earn a living, and the Government would give him from six to twelve dollars per month.

February 14   Daniel Manning resigned from post of Secretary of the Treasury, effective April 1.

February 16	Vetoed Texas Seed bill, indicating that this bill had good charitable intentions, but he doubted its constitutionality.
February 23	Importation of opium from China prohibited.
	House of Representatives passed Canada Retailiation Bill.
March 2	Hatch Act for the promotion of agricultural science became law. It provided federal subsidies for the creation of state agricultural experiment stations.
March 3	The Tenure of Office Act of April 5, 1869 was repealed because of Cleveland's contest with the Senate over appointments and removals from office.
March 22	Appointed Interstate Commerce Commissioners: Thomas M. Cooley of Michigan, William R. Morrison of Illinois, Augustus Schoonmaker of New York, Aldace F. Walker of Vermont, and Walter L. Bragg of Alabama.
April 1	Charles Stebbins Fairchild appointed Secretary of the Treasury.
April 28	Issued the famous order to Secretary Lamar regarding Guilford Miller's farm whereby railroad claims to land had to be surrendered if they were overdue. Called for justice to the unprotected settler.
April 30	Adjutant-General Drum wrote to Cleveland concerning the return of all Union and Confederate flags being stored at the War Department.
May 12	Presided at unveiling of Garfield Statue in Washington.
May 26	Endorsed proposal to return the Confederate flags.
June 7	Grand Army of the Republic indicated hostility toward returning captured Confederate flags to Southern States and criticized Cleveland for this act.
June 16	Withdrew approval for return of Confederate flags.
July 7	Withdrew acceptance of invitation to visit the Grand Army of the Republic National Convention in September because of deliberate insults to the President.

July 13   Delivered address at Centennial Celebration of the settlement of Clinton, New York.

July 19   Spoke at Manlius, New York.

July 21   Ohio Democratic Convention came out for a tariff only for purposes of producing a revenue enough to meet the expenses of an "economical administration" of the government. Other Western states took similar action.

August 9   Colorado troops battled Ute Indians.

**September
16-17**   Made several addresses in Philadelphia in honor of the Constitutional Centennial.

**September 30—
October 22**   Western and Southern tour.

December 6   Annual Message to Congress unique in that it was devoted solely to the tariff. Made a sweeping indictment of the tariff system.

1888

January 16   Lucius Quintus Cincinnatus Lamar of Mississippi appointed Associate Justice of the Supreme Court.

                   William Freeman Vilas of Wisconsin appointed Secretary of the Interior.

                   Donald McDonald Dickinson of Michigan appointed Postmaster General.

January 17   Submitted the two reports of the three commissioners who investigated the affairs of those railroads which received aid from the Government.

February 2   Submitted revised Civil Service rules.

February 20   Submitted Fisheries Treaty between Great Britain and the United States to the Senate. Was an agreement concerning the rights of American fishermen in Canadian waters, as well as duties to be charged on Canadian fish.

February 21-24 President and Mrs. Cleveland visited Florida.

March 21 Sent letter to United States Civil Service Commission requesting uniform classification in the Departments.

March 23 Chief Justice of the Supreme Court Morrison R. Waite died.

April 17 Roger Q. Mills introduced tariff bill into the House of Representatives. "The great tariff debate of 1888" began.

April 28 United States war vessels **Yorktown** and **Vesuvius** were launched. These ships were part of the "Steel Navy" program developed by Secretary of the Navy William C. Whitney in which he helped to revamp the United States Navy.

April 30 Melville W. Fuller nominated for Chief Justice.

May 30 Massachusetts was the first state to adopt the Australian or secret ballot.

June 5-7 Democratic National Convention at St. Louis, Missouri, nominated President Cleveland for re-election and Allen Granberry Thurman of Ohio for Vice-President.

June 13 Department of Labor established.

June 19-23 Republican National Convention at Chicago, Illinois, nominated Benjamin Harrison of Indiana for President and Levi Parsons Morton of New York for Vice-President.

July 20 Melville Weston Fuller of Illinois confirmed as Chief Justice of the Supreme Court.

July 23 Delivered the Fourth Report of the United States Civil Service Commission to Congress in which he traced the development of the Commission since the inception of civil service reform.

August Canadian fisheries issue caught the attention of the nation. President Cleveland had three aims: 1. To induce the Canadians to take a milder view toward New England fishermen in her waters. 2. To negotiate a treaty which would permanently settle the question. 3. If retaliation was necessary because of the failure of negotiations, retaliation was to be placed on an unselfish and national plane.

August 21   Treaty between the United States and Great Britain concerning fishing rights rejected by the Senate: 27 yeas to 30 nays.

August 23   Sent message to Congress concerning the Canadian fisheries problem, recommending retaliation upon Canada.

September 8   Delivered speech at Washington, D.C., accepting nomination for President.

October 1   Act passed providing for voluntary arbitration of railway disputes. The President was to appoint a commission to investigate any labor quarrel.

October 8   Signed Chinese Exclusion Act which issued regulations in regard to the exclusion of Chinese laborers.

October 24   Republicans published "Murchison Letter" from British Minister Sackville-West to "Charles Murchison," a naturalized Englishman (in reality George A. Osgoodby, a Republican). Sackville-West had urged that a vote for Cleveland was a vote for Britain. Cleveland demanded that the Minister be recalled. This was done on October 30.

October 31   Indianapolis **Sentinel** published the famous "Blocks-of-five Circular" sent out by the Republican National Treasurer W. W. Dudley, instructing party agents to purchase votes keeping them in blocks of five to be used where necessary. The Democrats did not use the issue to their advantage.

November 6   Cleveland defeated in the election. Benjamin Harrison, President-elect. Harrison received a total of 5,540,365 votes winning 233 electoral votes. Cleveland received 5,445,269 votes winning 168 electoral votes.

November 12   The United States Supreme Court affirmed the right of the Government to bring suit to annul the Bell Telephone patent.

December 8	Postmaster General Vilas placed the railway post-office employees under the Civil Service Law.

1889

January 16	Sent account to Congress of his efforts to protect American interests in Samoa. The Germans were trying to establish sovereignty over the archipelago.
February 1	Extradition Treaty with Great Britain rejected by the Senate.
February 7	Visited New York. Spoke with Francis Lynde Stetson about connection with firm of Banks, Stetson, and Company.
February 11	Signed bill establishing the Department of Agriculture.
February 13	Norman Jay Colman, Missouri, appointed to newly created post of Secretary of Agriculture.
February 22	Signed the territorial bill to admit North and South Dakota, Montana, and Washington as States.
	Delivered address at Georgetown University, where he conferred the Honorary Degrees at the Centennial Celebration.
March 4	Benjamin Harrison inaugurated as President of the United States.

INTERLUDE—OUT OF OFFICE

1889

March 7	Arrived in New York, residing at Victoria Hotel.
April 29	Conference over Samoan Affairs between Great Britain, Germany, and the United States began at Berlin.
April 30	Spoke at the Centennial Anniversary Dinner of the Nation's Birth in New York.
May 13	United States Supreme Court affirmed constitutionality of the Chinese Exclusion Act.
Summer	At Buzzard's Bay, Massachusetts.

July 4	Conventions to form State Constitution met in North Dakota, South Dakota, Montana and Washington Territories.
November 3	North Dakota and South Dakota admitted to the Union.
November 8	Montana admitted to the Union.
November 11	Washington admitted to the Union.
December 12	Delivered first public address to the Merchants' Association of Boston on ballot reform.

1890

Alfred Thayer Mahan published his influential work **The Influence of Sea Power upon History, 1660-1783.**

February 4	The Samoan Treaty with Germany and Great Britain was ratified by the Senate.
February 10	President Harrison declared the Sioux Reservation in South Dakota open to settlement.
February 15	Addressed the Bellevue Medical College Alumni in New York on the relationship between medicine and law.
February 22	Addressed the Southern Society of New York on "The Birthday of George Washington," urging that many fine traditions be kept.
March 6	Addressed a Public Meeting called by the Trustees of the New York Free Circulating Library on education and reading.
April 24	Addressed the Banquet of Piano and Organ Manufacturers' Association of the United States in New York on "Our American Industries."
June 27	President Harrison signed the Dependent Pension Act which Cleveland had vetoed on February 11, 1887.
July 3	Idaho admitted to the Union.
July 11	Wyoming admitted to the Union.

July 14 — Sherman Silver Purchase Act, sponsored by Senator John T. Sherman, signed by President Harrison.

October — Only ex-President to argue before the Supreme Court. Minor case which concerned the financial liability of New Orleans in a drainage project. 5-3 decision against Cleveland.

October 1 — President Harrison signed the McKinley Tariff raising tariff duties.

November — Elections in which the Democrats won control of the House of Representatives.

December 23 — Delivered address at the Reform Club Dinner. "The Campaign of Education; Its Result is a Signal Tribute to the Judgment of the American People."

1891

January 8 — Delivered address at the Young Men's Democratic Association of Philadelphia on the annual celebration of the Battle of New Orleans—perhaps his best speech.

January 24 — Delivered address at a public meeting sponsored by the New York State Forestry Association to endorse new legislation for the Adirondack Park.

February 10 — Sent letter to E. Ellery Anderson of the Reform Club stating that although he could not attend a dinner meeting to protest against free coinage, he was in favor of their views. He indicated that there would be great peril if a policy of unlimited coinage of silver were followed.

April 13 — Delivered address at the Democratic Club of New York on the anniversary of Thomas Jefferson's birthday.

May 12 — Delivered address at a reception tendered him by the "Cleveland Democracy" in Buffalo.

September 22 — New lands in Oklahoma opened to settlers.

October 3 — Ruth Cleveland born, New York City.

October 8 — Presided at Democratic mass meeting in Cooper Union, New York City. Looked toward tariff reform.

October 31	Delivered address in Boston in support of Governor Russell who was running for reelection.
December 12	Sent letter to William S. Bissell—a signal for organizing his campaign for the nomination.

1892

Published **Principles and Purposes of Our Form of Government.**

Published **Writings and Speeches of Grover Cleveland.**

February 22	New York State Democratic Convention ("Snap Convention") called at Albany. Stacked so as to foster Governor David Hill's plan to gain support for himself as the Democratic candidate for President.
	The People's Party of the U.S.A. (Populist) organized at St. Louis.
	Delivered address at the University of Michigan on "Sentiment in Our National Life."
March 1	United States Supreme Court confirmed the constitutionality of the McKinley Tariff Act.
March 9	Sent letter to Edmund S. Bragg discussing his interest in the nation and the Presidency, thereby indicating that he would be a candidate for President.
March 29	The Senate ratified the Bering Sea arbitration treaty without opposition.
April 2	Delivered address at Providence, Rhode Island on tariff reform.
April 21	United States invited other nations to a monetary conference.
June 7-10	Republican National Convention at Minneapolis, Minnesota, nominated President Benjamin Harrison for reelection and Whitelaw Reid of New York for Vice-President.
June 9	William Whitney brought together a "Conference" of national leaders of the Democratic Party, comprising a dozen representatives from ten states in support of Cleveland.

June 21-23	Democratic National Convention at Chicago, Illinois, nominated Grover Cleveland for President and Adlai Ewing Stevenson of Illinois for Vice-President.
July 2-5	People's Party of America Convention at Omaha, Nebraska, nominated James Blair Weaver of Iowa for President and James Gaven Field of Virginia for Vice-President.
July 6	Conflict between strikers at Carnegie Steel Works at Homestead, Pennsylvania and Pinkerton men. This private army had been organized by Henry Clay Frick, manager of the plant. The struggle resulted in ten killed and many wounded.
July 9	Governor Pattison of Pennsylvania ordered State troops into Homestead to preserve order.
July 20	Grover Cleveland accepted the Democratic nomination at the Notification Ceremony at Madison Square Garden in New York.
September 8-9	Victoria Hotel Conference in New York City brought Governor David Hill (Senator-elect) and Tammany forces back into Cleveland camp.
October 6	Delivered address at Buffalonian Cleveland Club in New York.
October 27	Delivered address at German American Cleveland Club at Cooper Union.
November 1	Delivered address at Business Men's Democratic Association in New York.
November 4	Delivered address at a Democratic mass meeting in Jersey City, New Jersey.
November 8	Cleveland elected President. Cleveland received a total of 5,556,982 votes winning 277 electoral votes and Harrison received 5,191,466 votes winning 145 electoral votes.
November 20	The Amalgamated Association declared strike at Homestead at an end.

December 10   Delivered address at Reform Club in New York, celebrating the Democratic victory.

1893

January 16   Revolution broke out in Hawaii. Sanford B. Dole had led the Americans in forming a revolutionary committee. U.S. Minister John L. Stevens ordered American marines to be landed from the cruiser **Boston,** ostensibly to protect American life and property, but actually to aid the revolutionists.

January 17   Ex-President Rutherford B. Hayes died. Cleveland attended funeral.

February 1   American Protectorate proclaimed in Hawaii.

February 15   President Harrison sent Treaty of Annexation of Hawaii to the Senate, which refused to act on it because of Democratic opposition.

February 24   Philadelphia & Reading Railroad, with debts of more than $125 million, went bankrupt.

SECOND TERM IN OFFICE

1893

March 4   Inaugurated. Chief Justice Weston Fuller administered the oath.

March 6   Cabinet Appointments: Secretary of State Walter Quintin Gresham of Illinois, Secretary of the Treasury John Griffin Carlisle of Kentucky, Secretary of War Daniel Scott Lamont of New York, Attorney General Richard Olney of Massachusetts, Postmaster General Wilson Shannon Bissell of New York, Secretary of the Navy Hilary Abner Herbert of Alabama, Secretary of the Interior Hoke Smith of Georgia, and Secretary of Agriculture Julius Sterling Morton of Nebraska.

March 9   Withdrew the Treaty of Annexation of Hawaii. Dispatched James H. Blount to Honolulu as Special Commissioner to investigate conditions in Hawaii.

March 20   Minister Bayard made Ambassador to England. He was the first American to receive this rank.

April 13	American Protectorate in Hawaii ended.
April 22	For the first time since its establishment the Gold Reserve in the Treasury fell below $100 million.
April 23	In a statement to the United Press said that the Executive and his Cabinet had every intention of maintaining the public credit and of preserving parity between gold and silver.
April 28	Reviewed Naval Ceremony in New York.
May 1	Opened World's Columbian Exposition in Chicago (Chicago World's Fair).
May 4	The National Cordage Company, whose stock was heavily inflated and had just paid a 100 per cent dividend in January, depreciated heavily. The Stock Market sunk, rallied feebly, and then went down to a new low point. This was the beginning of the Great Panic which spread throughout the nation.
May 8	Issued an Executive Order concerning the problem of interviews with the President whereby he would no longer meet with prospective office-holders and visitors.
May 15	Supreme Court declared the Geary Chinese Exclusion Act constitutional.
June	Early in month the Infanta Eulalia of the Spanish Royal Family visited Washington, where she was received at the White House.
June 18	White House Physician, Dr. R. M. O'Reilly examined the roof of Cleveland's mouth and found a malignant growth.
June 30	Issued Proclamation calling an Extraordinary Session of Congress, August 1.
July 1	Operation to remove part of the President's upper jaw, performed aboard Commodore E. C. Benedict's yacht in order to prevent the news from creating a greater financial panic.

July 11	Report sent by James H. Blount regarding Hawaii. Premature publication forced by leakage in November. Left no doubt that on moral and legal grounds the Treaty of Annexation was unjustified. Cleveland accepted it as final.
August 3	Currency was bought and sold at a premium in New York City.
August 7	Special Session of Congress opened.
August 8	Special Message read to Congress demanding repeal of provisions of the Act of July 14, 1890 authorizing the purchase of silver bullion.
August 11	Representative William L. Wilson of West Virginia opened debate on the Administration bill for repeal of the silver-purchase clauses.
August 15	Bering Sea Court of Arbitration denied the right of the United States to a closed sea.
August 16	William Jennings Bryan made a strong and impressionable speech in favor of free silver in the House of Representatives.
August 26	Thomas B. Reed, Speaker of the House of Representatives, delivered an eloquent speech in favor of sound money.
August 28	House of Representatives voted to repeal the silver-purchasing clauses of the Sherman Act, rejecting all free-coinage amendments.
September 5	Opened the Pan-American Medical Congress in Washington.
September 9	Esther Cleveland born. First child to be born in the White House.
September 16	The Cherokee Strip was opened for public settlement.
September 25	Published letter to Governor W. J. Northern of Georgia in which he stated that he wanted a sound currency so that those who have money will spend it.

October 18	Secretary of State Gresham presented Cleveland and his Cabinet with a full report on the Hawaiian situation with a plan of action. He recommended restoring Queen Lili-ukalani to power although existing circumstances prevented this method.
November 1	Sherman Silver Purchase Act repealed.
November 21	United States Supreme Court declared the Great Lakes to be high seas.
December 18	Delivered Special Message to Congress concerning the situation in Hawaii, revealing his desire to respect the wishes of the Hawaiians.
December 19	William L. Wilson introduced tariff bill to the House of Representatives. It was a moderate, perhaps even conservative piece, of legislation.

1894

January 17	First bond sale begun to replenish the Treasury's supply of gold.
February 1	Tariff Bill passed the House of Representatives.
February 19	Edward Douglass White, Louisiana, appointed Associate Justice of the United States Supreme Court.
March 15	Bland coinage bill passed by the Senate.
March 25	Jacob Coxey's Army began march from Massilon, Ohio, because of great financial misery. They were joined by contingents from other cities. They decreased in number before they reached Washington.
March 29	Vetoed Bland Bill for coining silver seigniorage and other loose bullion in the Treasury.
April 10	Issued the Bering Sea Proclamation.
April 21	Great strike in the soft coal fields began and spread to other areas and industries.
April 28	"Army of the Commonwealth of Christ" (Coxey's Army)

reached Washington quite depleted. Most of the men were arrested for trampling on the grass at the Capitol.

May Pullman strike broke out after the miserable winter of 1893-94, when Pullman Company announced twenty per cent reduction in the wages of its employees.

June 8 Signed the New York and New Jersey Bridge bill.

June 25 Boycott declared by the American Railway Union against the Pullman Palace Car Company, which resulted in the stopping of railroad traffic in the West and affected nearly 50,000 miles of railroads.

June 29 Proofs of armor plate frauds on United States naval vessels were obtained by Government, implicating the Carnegie Company.

July 2 Injunction issued by Federal Court against Eugene V. Debs, head of the American Railway Union, and strikers.

July 3 Dispatched Federal troops from Fort Sheridan to Chicago, Illinois, to maintain order and insure the transportation of mail during the strike of the employees of Pullman Palace Car Company and the sympathetic strike of railway workers. Arrived July 4.

Tariff Bill, after undergoing many changes, finally passed by Senate. Sent to Conference Committee.

July 4 Hawaii proclaimed itself a Republic.

July 5 Governor John P. Altgeld of Illinois protested sending of Federal troops into Chicago.

July 6 United States Deputy Marshals at Kensington, near Chicago, fired on strikers, killing two men and injuring others. Much railroad property was burned by mobs in Chicago.

July 8 Issued Proclamation to keep order in Chicago establishing martial law.

July 10 Eugene V. Debs and other railway union leaders indicted and arrested for obstructing the mails.

July 13   American Railway Union strike was ended.

Issued Proclamation putting into effect "An Act to adopt regulations for preventing collisions at sea" which had been approved August 19, 1890 and amended by Act of May 28, 1894.

July 17   Signed Enabling Act setting in motion Utah's statehood, prohibiting polygamy.

August 9   Hawaiian Republic officially recognized by United States Government.

August 13   House of Representatives passed the revised tariff bill under the sponsorship of William L. Wilson and Arthur Pue Gorman.

August 18   Carey Act passed, providing for land reclamation by irrigation.

August 28   Wilson-Gorman Tariff bill, including an income tax amendment, became law without the President's signature. The tax amendment taxed income on stocks and bonds.

November 6   Congressional elections. Republicans gained control of House of Representatives.

November 14   Second bond sale announced. Bids to be opened November 24. Gave the Treasury $50,000 more from a successful syndicate than the aggregate of the highest offers.

December 1   Secretary Gresham instructed Ambassador Bayard to open the question of the Venezuelan boundary with the British Government.

December 9   New treaty between the United States and Japan was proclaimed.

December 14   Eugene V. Debs was sentenced to six months' imprisonment for contempt of court during the great railroad strike.

1895

January 28   Gold supply had again dwindled. Sent Special Message to Congress making a last appeal requesting that legislation be enacted to prevent the complete depletion of the gold supply in the Treasury.

February 6   As arbitrator in the boundary dispute between Brazil and the Argentine Republic, Cleveland decided in favor of Brazil.

February 8   Gold reserve less than five per cent of traditional level of safety. Delivered Special Message announcing that arrangements had been made for the third bond issue to be purchased by a syndicate led by J.P. Morgan.

February 20   The Morgan syndicate sold the bonds at a nice profit.

Joint Congressional resolution approved Cleveland's recommendation that Great Britain and Venezuela submit their boundary disputes to arbitration.

February 24   Cuban Revolt began.

February 27   Postmaster General Bissell resigned.

March 1   William Lyne Wilson of West Virginia appointed Postmaster General, assuming duties April 4.

April 13   Addressed letter to a Chicago group who had invited him to speak at a sound money gathering. Warned against wild experiments; sound currency was most important.

April 29   In a letter to Governor J. M. Stone of Mississippi, said that the Democratic Party must remain true to its traditional doctrine of sound and safe money or it will go down to defeat.

May 20   **Pollock v. Farmers' and Trust Company.** 157 U.S. 429 (1895) and 158 U.S. 601 (1895). Supreme Court nullified the income tax provision of the Wilson-Gorman tariff.

May 23   Secretary Carlisle spoke against the free coinage of silver at the Sound Money Convention at Memphis.

May 27   **In re Debs.** 158 U.S. 564 (1895). Supreme Court ruled that injunctions could be issued against any action that threatened the general welfare.

May 28   Secretary of State Walter Quintin Gresham died at Washington.

June 8   Richard Olney, Attorney General, appointed Secretary of

State, assuming his duties June 10.

Judson Harmon of Ohio appointed Attorney General, entered upon duties June 11.

June 12   Issued proclamation against Cuban filibusters.

July 7   Marion Cleveland born at Buzzards Bay, Massachusetts.

July 20   Secretary of State Olney sent belligerent note to British Government indicating that peaceful arbitration was the only method to solve the Venezuelan boundary dispute. Pressure would be regarded as a violation of the Monroe Doctrine by the United States.

August 14   Senators David Turpie of Indiana, James K. Jones of Arkansas, and Isham G. Harris of Tennessee called for a conference of prominent Democrats from all over the country at Washington, D.C., to establish a silver organization within the party. After the meeting the silver crusade spread like wildfire.

September 19   National Park on the site of the Chickamauga battleground, Tennessee, dedicated by a great gathering of Union and Confederate veterans.

October 22   Visited the Atlanta Exposition with members of his Cabinet.

November 26   British Prime Minister Lord Salisbury answered the Olney note of July 20, claiming that the Monroe Doctrine was not applicable to the boundary dispute and rejecting the American offer of arbitration.

December 9   Appointed Rufus William Peckham of New York Associate Justice of the Supreme Court.

December 17   Delivered Special Message to Congress denouncing Great Britain's refusal to consent to arbitration with Venezuela in the territorial dispute between Venezuela and British Guiana. He requested that Congress appropriate the money for a commission to determine the true Venezuelan boundary, and declared that it would be the duty of the United States to maintain the boundary against any aggresion.

December 20   Delivered Special Message to Congress in regard to depletion of gold from the Treasury.

1896

January 1   Announced the members of the Venezuelan Boundary Commission: David J. Brewer of Kansas, Richard G. Alvey of Maryland, Andrew D. White of New York, Frederic R. Coudert of New York, and Daniel G. Gilman of Maryland.

January 4   Issued Proclamation declaring Utah a state of the Union.

January 6   Secretary Carlisle announced the fourth bond issue of $100 million to be sold publicly. J. P. Morgan's syndicate purchased almost $35 million.

February   By end of month gold reserve had reached $124 million. The bond sale was successful.

April   Sent Carlisle to Chicago to counteract Governor Altgeld's influence and win labor to the gold standard.

May 1   In a letter to Don M. Dickinson of Michigan, stated that he felt that the Democratic Party must follow the example of Michigan in standing for sound money.

May 6   Issued a revision of the Civil Service Rules.

June 16   Addressed letter to Democratic voters, published in the New York **Herald,** urging sound money and speaking strongly against free, unlimited, and independent coinage of silver.

June 16-18   Republican National Convention at St. Louis, Missouri, nominated William McKinely of Ohio for President and Garret Augustus Hobart of New Jersey for Vice-President.

July 7-11   Democratic National Convention at Chicago, Illinois, repudiated Cleveland and his administration. Nominated William Jennings Bryan of Nebraska for President and Arthur Sewall of Maine for Vice-President.

July 13   Honest Money League of Chicago issued declaration to Democrats of the nation denouncing the National Convention that had just ended.

July 20   Secretary of the Interior Hoke Smith wrote to President that he is endorsing Bryan because he will not go against the Party.

July 27   Issued another proclamation against Cuban filibusters.

August 7   Gold Democrats met at Indianapolis in an attempt to try to defeat Bryan.

August 22   Hoke Smith resigned post as Secretary of the Interior.

September 1   David Rowland Francis of Missouri appointed Secretary of the Interior, assuming his duties September 4.

September 3   Addressed letter to Daniel G. Griffin, Chairman of the New York Delegation of the National Democratic (Gold) Party that he would not accept the nomination of this Party.

October 22   Delivered address at Sesquicentennial celebration of the College of New Jersey, which on this date took the name of Princeton University.

November 3   William McKinley elected President. McKinley received a total of 7,113,734 votes winning 271 electoral votes, and Bryan received 6,516,722 votes winning 176 electoral votes.

November 8   Cleveland addressed letter to Professor Andrew F. West asking for information about Princeton, where he would like to settle after March 4.

November 16   In a letter to Alexander E. Orr, President of the United States Chamber of Commerce, urged that there must be thorough reforms in the financial system.

December 31   Issued Proclamation putting into effect regulations for the prevention of collisions at sea as arranged by the Acts of August 19, 1890, and June 10, 1896.

1897
Published **Self Made Man in American Life.**

January 11   Treaty of Arbitration between the United States and Great Britain was signed at Washington by Secretary Olney and Ambassador Julian Pauncefote.

February 2   Treaty between Great Britain and Venezuela providing for submission of their dispute to arbitration signed at State Department in Washington.

February 9   Bill to regulate immigration passed by House of Represenatives after being passed by Senate. Vetoed by President.

RETIREMENT

1897

March 4   Participated in inaugural ceremonies of William McKinley as President.

March 18   Arrived in Princeton, where he was to settle for the remainder of his life.

May 5   Senate rejected Treaty of Arbitration with Great Britain.

June 14   Venezuela Boundary Treaty between Great Britain and Venezuela ratified at Washington. President Cleveland had worked hard to achieve this important agreement and Benjamin Harrison had also been involved in this momentous conclusion of a serious riff between the two nations.

September 14   Hawaiian Senate unanimously ratified a treaty of annexation with the United States.

October 3   Venezuelan Arbitration Commission made award, which was in substantial accord with the original British claims.

October 28   Richard Folsom Cleveland born at Princeton, New Jersey.

1898

February 15   United States battleship **Maine** blown up in Havana Harbor.

April 25   War declared by Congress upon Spain.

June 16   The Treaty for the annexation of Hawaii was passed by both Houses of Congress under a joint resolution to preclude its defeat under the two-thirds vote required for treaty ratification in the Senate. Cleveland had blocked all attempts to annex the Hawaiian Islands while he was in office and still did not approve of this act.

1899

February 6   Senate ratified the Treaty of Paris with Spain ending the war.

1900

Published **Independence of the Executive.**

April 9-10   Delivered two lectures at Princeton University on "The Independence of the Executive."

June 19   Republican National Convention at Philadelphia, Pennsylvania, nominated President William McKinley for reelection and Theodore Roosevelt of New York for Vice-President.

July 4   Democratic National Convention at Kansas City, Missouri, nominated William Jennings Bryan for President, and Adlai E. Stevenson of Illinois for Vice-President.

October 12   In a letter to Don M. Dickinson indicated that although he could not support Bryan he would not condone the formation of a third party.

November 6   President McKinley reelected. McKinley received a total of 7,219,828 votes winning 292 electoral votes, and Bryan received 6,357,100 votes winning 155 electoral votes.

1901

March 27-28   Delivered two lectures at Princeton University on the Venezuelan Boundary Dispute.

September 6   President McKinley shot at Buffalo, New York.

September 14   After a long period of suffering, President McKinley died. Theodore Roosevelt took the oath as President.

October 15   Cleveland elected a trustee of Princeton University.

May 12   United Mine Workers of America led 45,000 miners on strike when the mine owners declined an offer of arbitration.

October 3   President Roosevelt called a conference at the White House between the presidents of the anthracite coal companies and John Mitchell, President of the United Mine Workers of America.

October 4   Cleveland suggested in a letter to President Roosevelt a method for getting the miners back to work pending negotiations. They would produce enough coal for the consumers and then continue discussions. As result President Roosevelt asked him to head the Arbitration Commission. Did not eventually participate. The President appointed the Commission on October 16.

October 21   United Mine Workers ended strike. The Commission awarded the workers a wage increase of ten per cent on March 22, 1903, although it refused union recognition.

1903

February 6   In a letter to Joseph Garretson, editor of the Cincinnati Times-Star, indicated that he did not see enough sentiment for him to think of accepting the Democratic nomination for President. This led to an erroneous assumption that he might submit if the pressure were strong enough.

April 14   Delivered address in New York on the industrial education of the Southern Negro.

April 30   Delivered address at the Louisiana Purchase Exposition at St. Louis on the importance of conservation and forestry.

July 18   Francis Grover Cleveland born at Buzzards Bay, Massachusetts. Fifth and last child.

November 25   In a letter to Dr. St. Clair Mckelway indicated that he could not be a candidate for the presidency and gave permission to publish this information.

1904

January 7   Eldest daughter, Ruth, died.

May 2   Delivered lecture at Princeton University on the Chicago strike.

June 26   Addressed letter to James Smith, Jr., head of the New Jersey delegation to the Democratic Convention, to prevent his name from being mentioned for President.

October   Published **Presidential Problems,** compilation of lectures given at Princeton University from 1901 to 1904.

October 21   Delivered address in New York. First campaign speech for Alton B. Parker, Democratic nominee for President.

November 4   Delivered address at Newark. Second and last campaign appearance.

1905

January 29   Delivered address at the Fiftieth Anniversary of the Philadelphia YMCA providing a moral guide for the Nation: "Inviolable Good Faith, Love of Peace, Truth, and Justice."

June 10   Accepted position as one of three trustees to hold the stock and supervise the reorganization of the Equitable Life Assurance Society, which had been acquired by Thomas F. Ryan. Stock transferred by June 15. The Society was reorganized by the end of June.

December 19   Accepted position as a referee in matters of dispute among the New York Life Insurance Company, the Mutual Life Company and the Equitable Life Assurance Society.

1907

February   "The Presidents' Association of Life Insurance Companies" formed. Urged Cleveland to take the post as the head of the organization, which he did accept.

1908
Published **Good Citizenship**

April   Cleveland's strength had been ebbing for several years. He was in the grip of a gastro-intestinal disease complicated by heart and kidney ailments.

June 24   After a series of attacks, died at Princeton.

June 26   Buried at Princeton.

DOCUMENTS

FIRST INAUGURAL ADDRESS
March 4, 1885

In this address Cleveland called for political and sectional unity. He indicated a need for reform of the financial system and the administration of the government, protection of the public domain and the Indians, as well as strict enforcement of the immigration laws.

Fellow Citizens:

In the presence of this vast assemblage of my countrymen I am about to supplement and seal by the oath which I shall take the manifestation of the will of a great and free people. In the exercise of their power and right of self-government they have committed to one of their fellow-citizens a supreme and sacred trust, and he here consecrates himself in their service.

This impressive ceremony adds little to the solemn sense of responsibility with which I contemplate the duty I owe to all the people of the land. Nothing can relieve me from anxiety lest by any act of mine their interests may suffer, and nothing is needed to strengthen my resolution to engage every faculty and effort in the promotion of their welfare.

Amid the din of party strife the people's choice was made, but its attendant circumstances have demonstrated anew the strength and safety of a government by the people. In each succeeding year it more clearly appears that our democratic principle needs no apology, and that in its fearless and faithful application is to be found the surest guaranty of good government. . . .

To-day the executive branch of the Government is transferred to new keeping. But this is still the Government of the people, and it should be none the less an object of their affectionate solicitude. At this hour the animosities of political strife, the bitterness of partisan defeat, and the exultation of partisan triumph should be supplanted by an ungrudging acquiescence in the popular will and a sober, conscientious concern for the general weal. Moreover, if from this hour we cheerfully and honestly abandon all sectional prejudice and distrust, and determine, with manly confidence in one another, to work out harmoniously the achievements of our national destiny, we shall deserve to realize all the benefits which our happy form of government can bestow.

On this auspicious occasion we may well renew the pledge of devotion to the Constitution, which, launched by the founders of the Republic and consecrated by their prayers and patriotic devotion, has for almost a century borne the hopes and the aspirations of a great people through prosperity and peace and through the shock of foreign conflicts and the perils of domestic strife and vicissitudes.

By the Father of his Country our Constitution was commended for adoption as "the result of a spirit of amity and mutual concession." In that same spirit it should be administered, in order to promote the lasting welfare of the country and to secure the full measure of its priceless benefits to us and to those who will succeed to the blessings of our national life. The large variety of diverse and competing interests subject to Federal control, persistently seeking the recognition of their claims, need give us no fear that "the greatest good to the greatest number" will fail to be accomplished if in the halls of national legislation that spirit of amity and mutual concession shall prevail in which the Constitution had its birth. If this involves the surrender or postponement of private interests and the abandonment of local advantages, compensation will be found in the assurance that the common interest is subserved and the general welfare advanced.

In the discharge of my official duty I shall endeavor to be guided by a just and unstrained construction of the Constitution, a careful observance of the distinction between the powers granted to the Federal Government and those reserved to the States or to the people, and by a cautious appreciation of those functions which by the Constitution and laws have been especially assigned to the executive branch of the Government.

But he who takes the oath to-day to preserve, protect, and defend the Constitution of the United States only assumes the solemn obligation which every patriotic citizen—on the farm, in the workshop, in the busy marts of trade, and everywhere—should share with him. The Constitution which prescribes his oath, my countrymen, is yours; the Government you have chosen him to administer for a time is yours; the suffrage which executes the will of freemen is yours; the laws and the entire scheme of our civil rule, from the town meeting to the State capitals and the national capital, is yours. Your every voter, as surely as your Chief Magistrate, under the same high sanction, though in a different sphere, exercises a public trust. Nor is this all. Every citizen owes to the country a vigilant watch and close scrutiny of its public servants and a fair and reasonable estimate of their fidelity and usefulness. Thus is the people's will impressed upon the whole framework of our civil polity—municipal, State, and Federal; and this is the price of our liberty and the inspiration of our faith in the Republic.

It is the duty of those serving the people in public place to closely limit public expenditures to the actual needs of the Government economically administered, because this bounds the right of the Government to exact tribute from the earnings of labor or the property of the citizen, and because public extravagance begets extravagance among the people.

Those who are selected for a limited time to manage public affairs are still of the people, and may do much by their example to encourage, consistently with the dignity of their official functions, that plain way of life which among their fellow-citizens aids integrity and promotes thrift and prosperity.

The genius of our institutions, the needs of our people in their home life, and the attention which is demanded for the settlement and development of the resources of our vast territory dictate the scrupulous avoidance of any departure from the foreign policy commended by the history, the traditions, and the prosperity of our Republic. It is the policy of independence favored by our position and defended by our known love of justice and by our power. It is the policy of peace suitable to our interests. It is the policy of neutrality, rejecting any share in foreign broils and ambitions upon other continents and repelling their intrusion here. It is the policy of Monroe and of Washington and Jefferson—"Peace, commerce, and honest friendship with all nations; entangling alliance with none."

A due regard for the interests and prosperity of all the people demands that our finances shall be established upon such a sound and sensible basis as shall secure the safety and confidence of business interests and make the wage of labor sure and steady, and that our system of revenue shall be so adjusted as to relieve the people of unnecessary taxation, having a due regard to the interests of capital invested and workingmen employed in American industries, and preventing the accumulation of a surplus in the Treasury to tempt extravagance and waste.

Care for the property of the nation and for the needs of future settlers requires that the public domain should be protected from purloining schemes and unlawful occupation.

The conscience of the people demands that the Indians within our boundaries shall be fairly and honestly treated as wards of the Government and their education and civilization promoted with a view to their ultimate citizenship and that polygamy in the Territories, destructive of the family relation and offensive to the moral sense of the civilized world, shall be repressed.

The laws should be rigidly enforced which prohibit the immigration of a servile class to compete with American labor, with no intention of acquiring citizenship, and bringing them and retaining habits and customs repugnant to our civilization.

The people demand reform in the administration of the Government and the application of business principle to public affairs. As a means to this end, civil-service reform should be in good faith enforced. Our citizens have the right to protection from the incompetency of public employees who hold their places solely as the reward of partisan service, and from the corrupting influence of those who promise and the vicious methods of those who expect such rewards; and those who worthily seek public employment have the right to insist that merit and competency shall be recognized instead of party subserviency or the surrender of honest political belief.

In the administration of a government pledged to do equal and exact justice to all men there should be no pretext for anxiety touching the protection of the freedmen in their rights or their security in the enjoyment of their privileges under the Constitution and its amendments. All discussion as to their fitness for the place accorded to them as American citizens is idle and unprofitable except as it suggests the necessity for their improvement. The fact that they are citizens entitles them to all the rights due to that relation and charges them with all its duties, obligations, and responsibilities.

These topics and the constant and ever-varying wants of an active and enterprising population may well receive the attention and the patriotic endeavor of all who make and excute the Federal law. Our duties are practical and call for industrious application, an intelligent perception of the claims of public office and, above all, a firm determination, by united action, to secure all the people of the land the full benefits of the best form of government ever vouchsafed to man. And let us not trust to human effort alone, but humbly acknowledging the power and goodness of Almighty God, who presides over the destiny of nations, and who has at all times been revealed in our country's history, let us invoke His aid and His blessing upon our labors.

March 4, 1885

SPECIAL MESSAGE TO CONGRESS:
PRESIDENTIAL APPOINTMENTS AND REMOVALS
March 1, 1886

*Facing great difficulties over the Tenure of Office Act
of 1869 and demands for information relating to the
removal of certain officers, Cleveland replied to the
Senate in this Message that this body is entitled
to the information only in regard to appointments. He
reserved his right as President to determine the type
of papers to be sent and to act as long as he remained
within the law.*

EXECUTIVE MANSION
Washington, D.C., March 1, 1886

To the Senate of the United States:

Ever since the beginning of the present session of the Senate the different heads of the Departments attached to the executive branch of the Government have been plied with various requests and demands from committees of the Senate, from members of such committees, and at last from the Senate itself, requiring the transmission of reasons for the suspension of certain officials during the recess of that body, or for all the papers touching the conduct of such officials, or for all papers and documents relating to such suspensions, or for all documents and papers in such Departments in relation to the management and conduct of the offices held by such suspended officials.

The different terms from time to time adopted in making these requests and demands, the order in which they succeeded each other, and that fact that when made by the Senate the resolution for that purpose was passed in executive session have led to the presumption, the correctness of which will, I suppose, be candidly admitted, that from the first to the last the information thus sought and the papers thus demanded were desired for use by the Senate and its committees in considering the propriety of the suspensions referred to.

Though these suspensions are my executive acts based upon considerations addressed to me alone and for which I am wholly responsible, I have had no invitation from the Senate to state the position which I have felt constrained to assume in relation to the same or to interpret for myself my acts and motives in the premises.

In this condition of affairs I have forborne addressing the Senate upon the subject, lest I might be accused of thrusting myself unbidden upon the attention of that body.

But the report of the Committee on the Judiciary of the Senate lately presented and published, which censures the Attorney-General of the United States for his refusal to transmit certain papers relating to a suspension from office, and which also, if I correctly interpret it, evinces a misapprehension of the position of the Executive upon the question of such suspensions, will, I hope, justify this communication.

This report is predicated upon a resolution of the Senate directed to the Attorney-General and his reply to the same. This resolution was adopted in executive session devoted entirely to business connected with the consideration of nominations for office. It required the Attorney-General "to transmit to the Senate copies of all documents and papers that have been filed in the Department of Justice since the 1st day of January, 1885, in relation to the management and conduct of the office of district attorney of the United States for the southern district of Alabama."

The incumbent of this office on the 1st day of January, 1885, and until the 17th day of July ensuing, was George M. Duskin, who on the day last mentioned was suspended by an Executive order, and John D. Burnett designated to perform the duties of said office. At the time of the passage of the resolution above referred to the nomination of Burnett for said office was pending before the Senate, and all the papers relating to said nomination were before that body for its inspection and information.

In reply to this resolution the Attorney-General, after referring to the fact that the papers relating to the nomination of Burnett had already been sent to the Senate, stated that he was directed by the President to say that—

> The papers and documents which are mentioned in said resolution and still remaining in the custody of this Department, having exclusive reference to the suspension by the President of George M. Duskin, the late incumbent of the office of district attorney for the southern district of Alabama, it is not considered that the public interests will be promoted by a compliance with said resolution and the transmission of the papers and documents therein mentioned to the Senate in executive session.

Upon this resolution and the answer thereto the issue is thus stated by the Committee on the Judiciary at the outset of the report:

> The important question, then, is whether it is within the constitutional competence of either House of Congress to have access to the official papers and documents in the various public offices of the United States created by laws enacted by themselves.

I do not suppose that "the public offices of the United States" are regulated or controlled in their relations to either House of Congress by the fact that they were "created by laws enacted by themselves." It must be that these instrumentalities were created for the benefit of the people and to answer the general purposes of government under the Con- stitution and the laws, and that they are unencumbered by any lien in favor of either branch of Congress growing out of their construction, and unembarrassed by any obligation to the Senate as the price of their creation.

The complaint of the committee that access to official papers in the public offices is denied the Senate is met by the statement that at no time has it been the disposition or the intention of the President or any Department of the executive branch of the Government to withhold from the Senate official documents or papers filed in any of the public offices. While it is by no means conceded that the Senate has the right in any case to review the act of the Executive in removing or suspending a public officer, upon official documents or otherwise, it is considered that documents and papers of that nature should, because they are offic- ial, be freely transmitted to the Senate upon its demand, trusting the use of the same for proper and legitimate purposes to the good faith of that body; and though no such paper or document has been specifically demanded in any of the numerous requests and demands made upon the Department, yet as often as they were found in the public offices they have been furnished in answer to such applications.

The letter of the Attorney-General in response to the resolution of the Senate in the particular case mentioned in the committee's report was written at my suggestion and by my direction. There had been no official papers or documents filed in his Department relating to the case within the period specified in the resolution. The letter was intended, by its description of the papers and documents remaining in the custody of the Department, to convey the idea that they were not official; and it was assumed that the resolution called for information, papers, and docu- ments remaining in the custody of the Department, to convey the idea that they were not official; and it was assumed that the resolution called for information, papers and documents of the same character as were required by the requests and demands which preceded it.

Everything that had been written or done on behalf of the Senate from the beginning pointed to all letters and papers of a private and unofficial nature as the objects of a search, if they were to be found in the Departments, and provided they had been presented to the Executive with a view to their consideration upon the question of suspension from office.

Against the transmission of such papers and documents I have inter- posed my advice and direction. This has not been done, as is suggested in the committee's report, upon the assumption on my part that the Attorney-General or any other head of a Department "is the servant of the President, and is to give or withhold copies of documents in his office according to the will of the Executive and not otherwise," but because I regard the papers and documents withheld and addressed to me or intended for my use and action purely unofficial and private, not infrequently confidential, and having reference to the performance of a duty exclusively mine. I consider them in no proper sense as upon the files of the Department, but as deposited there for my convenience, remaining still completely under my control. I suppose if I desired to take them into my custody I might do so with entire propriety, and if I saw fit to destroy them no one could complain.

Even the committee in its report appears to concede that there may be with the President or in the Department's papers and documents which, on account of their unofficial character are not subject to the inspection of the Congress. A reference in the report to instances where the House of Representatives ought not to succeed in a call for the production of papers is immediately followed by this statement:

The committee feels authorized to state, after a somewhat careful research, that within the foregoing limits there is scarcely in the history of this Government, until now, any instance of a refusal by a head of a Department, or even of the President himself, to communicate official facts and information, as distinguished from private and unofficial papers, motions, views, reasons, and opinions, to either House of Congress when unconditionally demanded.

To which of the classes thus recognized do the papers and documents belong that are now the objects of the Senate's quest?

They consist of letters and representations addressed to the Executive or intended for his inspection; they are voluntarily written and presented by private citizens who are not in the least instigated thereto by any official invitation or at all subject to official control. While some of them are entitled to Executive consideration, many of them are so irrelevant or in the light of other facts so worthless, that they have not been given the least weight in determining the question to which they are supposed to relate.

Are all these, simply because they are preserved, to be considered official documents and subject to the inspection of the Senate? If not, who is to determine which belong to this class? Are the motives and purposes of the Senate, as they are day by day developed, such as would be satisfied with my selection? Am I to submit to theirs at the risk of being charged with making a suspension from office upon evidence which was not even considered?

Are these papers to be regarded as official because they have not only been presented but preserved in the public offices?

Their nature and character remain the same whether they are kept in the Executive Mansion or deposited in the Departments. There is no mysterious power of transmutation in departmental custody, nor is there magic in the undefined and sacred solemnity of Department files. If the presence of these papers in the public offices is a stumbling block in the way of the performance of Senatorial duty, it can be easily removed.

The papers and documents which have been described derive no official character from any constitutional, statutory, or other requirement making them necessary to the performance of the official duty of the Executive.

It will not be denied, I suppose, that the President may suspend a public officer in the entire absence of any papers or documents to aid his official judgment and discretion; and I am quite prepared to avow that the cases are not few in which suspensions from office have depended more upon oral representations made to me by citizens of known good repute and by members of the House of Representatives and Senators of the United States than upon any letters and documents presented for my examination. I have not felt justified in suspecting the veracity, integrity and patriotism of Senators or ignoring their representations, because they were not in party affiliation with the majority of their associates; and I recall a few suspensions which bear the approval of individual members identified politically with the majority in the Senate.

While, therefore, I am constrained to deny the right of the Senate to the papers and documents described, so far as the right to the same as based upon the claim that they are in any view of the subject official, I am also led unequivocally to dispute the right of the Senate by the aid of any documents whatever, or in any way save through the judicial process of trial or impeachment, to review or reverse the acts of the Executive in the suspension, during the recess of the Senate, of Federal officials.

I believe the power to remove or suspend such officials is vested in the President alone by the Constitution, which in express terms provides that "the executive power shall be vested in a President of the United States of America," and that "he shall take care that the laws be faithfully executed."

The Senate belongs to the legislative branch of the Government. When the Constitution by express provision superadded to its legislative duties the right to advise and consent to appointments to office and to sit as a court of impeachment, it conferred upon that body all the control and regulation of Executive action supposed to be necessary for the safety of the people; and this express and special grant of such extraordinary powers, not in any way related to or growing out of general Senatorial duty, and in itself a departure from the general plan of our Government, should be held, under a familiar maxim of construction, to exclude every other right of interference with Executive functions.

In the first Congress which assembled after the adoption of the Constitution, comprising many who aided in its preparation, a legislative construction was given to that instrument in which the independence of the Executive in the matter of removals from office was fully sustained.

I think it will be found that in the subsequent discussions of this question there was generally, if not at all times, a proposition pending to in some way curtail this power of the President by legislation, which furnishes evidence that to limit such power it was supposed to be necessary to supplement the Constitution by such legislation.

The first enactment of this description was passed under a stress of partisanship and political bitterness which culminated in the President's impeachment.

This law provided that the Federal officers to which it applied could only be suspended during the recess of the Senate when shown by evidence satisfactory to the President to be guilty of misconduct in office, or crime, or when incapable or disqualified to perform their duties, and that within twenty days after the next meeting of the Senate it should be the duty of the President "to report to the Senate such suspension, with the evidence and reasons for his action in the case."

This statute, passed in 1867, when Congress was overwhelmingly and bitterly opposed to the President, may be regarded as an indication that even then it was thought necessary by a Congress determined upon the subjugation of the Executive to legislative will to furnish itself a law for that purpose, instead of attempting to reach the object intended by an invocation of any pretended constitutional right.

The law which thus found its way to our statute book was plain in its terms, and its intent needed no avowal. If valid and now in operation, it would justify the present course of the Senate and command the obedience of the Executive to its demands. It may, however, be remarked in passing that under this law the President had the privilege of presenting to the body which assumed to review his executive acts his reasons therefor, instead of being excluded from explanation or judged by papers found in the Departments.

Two years after the law of 1867 was passed, and within less than five weeks after the inauguration of a President in political accord with both branches of Congress, the sections of the act regulating suspensions from office during the recess of the Senate were entirely repealed, and in their place were substituted provisions, which, instead of limiting the causes of suspension to misconduct, crime, disability, or disqualification, expressly permitted such suspension by the President "in his discretion," and completely abandoned the requirement obliging him to report to the Senate "the evidence and reasons" for his action.

With these modifications and with all branches of the Government in political harmony, and in the absence of partisan incentive to captious obstruction, the law as it was left by the amendment of 1869 was much less destructive of Executive discretion. And yet the great general patriotic citizen who on the 4th day of March, 1869, assumed the duties of Chief Executive, and for whose freer administration of his high office the most hateful restraints of the law of 1867 were, on the 5th day of April, 1869, removed, mindful of his obligation to defend and protect every perogative of his great trust, and apprehensive of the injury threatened the public service in the continued operation of these statutes even in their modified form in his first message to Congress advised their repeal and set forth their unconstitutional character and hurtful tendency in the following language:

It may be well to mention here the embarrassment possible to arise from leaving on the statute books the so-called "tenure-of-office acts," and to earnestly recommend their total repeal. It could not have been the intention of the framers of the Constitution, when providing that appointments made by the President should receive the consent of the Senate, that the latter should have the power to retain in office persons placed there by Federal appointment against the will of the President. The law is inconsistent with a faithful and efficient administration of the Government. What faith can an Executive put in officials forced upon him, and those, too, whom he has suspended for reason? How will such officials be likely to serve an Administration which they know does not trust them?

I am unable to state whether or not this recommendation for a repeal of these laws has been since repeated. If it has not, the reason can probably be found in the experience which demonstrated the fact that the necessities of the political situation but rarely developed their vicious character.

And so it happens that after an existence of nearly twenty years of almost innocuous desuetude these laws are brought forth—apparently the repealed as well as the unrepealed—and put in the way of an Executive who is willing, if permitted, to attempt an improvement in the methods of administration.

The constitutionality of these laws is by no means admitted. But why should the provisions of the repealed law, which required specific cause for suspension and a report to the Senate of "evidence and reasons," be now in effect applied to the present Executive, instead of the law, afterwards passed and unrepealed, which distinctly permits suspensions by the President "in his discretion" and carefully omits the requirement that "evidence and reasons for his action in the case" shall be reported to the Senate.

The requests and demands which by the score have for nearly three months been presented to the different Departments of the Government, whatever may be their form, have but one complexion. They assume the right of the Senate to sit in judgment upon the exercise of my exclusive discretion and Executive functions, for which I am solely responsible to the people from whom I have so lately received the sacred trust of office. My oath to support and defend the Constitution, my duty to the people who have chosen me to execute the powers of their great office and not to relinquish them, and my duty to the Chief Magistracy, which I must preserve unimpaired in all its dignity and vigor, compel me to refuse compliance with these demands.

To the end that the service may be improved, the Senate is invited to the fullest scrutiny of the persons submitted to them for public office, in recognition of the constitutional power of that body to advise and consent to their appointment. I shall continue, as I have thus far done, to furnish at the request of the confirming body, all the information I possess touching the fitness of the nominees placed before them for their action, both when they are proposed to fill vacancies and to take the place of suspended officials. Upon a refusal to confirm I shall not assume the right to ask the reasons for the action of the Senate nor question its determination. I can not think that anything is required to secure worthy incumbents in public office than a careful and independent discharge of our respective duties within their well-defined limits.

Though the propriety of suspensions might be better assured if the action of the President was subject to review by the Senate, yet if the Constitution and the laws have placed this responsibility upon the executive branch of the Government it should not be divided nor the discretion which it involves relinquished.

It has been claimed that the present Executive having pledged himself not to remove officials except for cause, the fact of their suspension implies such misconduct on the part of a suspended official as injures his character and reputation, and therefore the Senate should review the case for his vindication.

I have said that certain officials should not, in my opinion, be removed during the continuance of the term for which they were appointed solely for the purpose of putting in their place those in political affiliation with the appointing power, and this declaration was immediately followed by a description of official partisanship which ought not to entitle those in whom it was exhibited to consideration. It is not apparent how an adherence to the course thus announced carries with it the consequences described. If in any degree the suggestion is worthy of consideration, it is to be hoped that there may be a defense against unjust suspension in the justice of the Executive.

Every pledge which I have made by which I have placed a limitation upon my exercise of executive power has been faithfully redeemed. Of course the pretense is not put forth that no mistakes have been committed; but not a suspension has been made except it appeared to my satisfaction that the public welfare would be improved thereby. Many applications for suspension have been denied, and the adherence to the rule laid down to govern my action as to such suspensions has caused much irritation and impatience on the part of those who have insisted upon more changes in the offices.

The pledges I have made were made to the people, and to them I am responsible for the manner in which they have been redeemed. I am not responsible to the Senate, and I am unwilling to submit my actions and official conduct to them for judgment.

There are no grounds for an allegation that the fear of being found false to my profession influences me in declining to submit to the demands of the Senate. I have not constantly refused to suspend officials, and thus incurred the displeasure of political friends, and yet willfully broken faith with the people for the sake of being false to them.

Neither the discontent of party friends, nor the allurement constantly offered of confirmation of appointees conditioned upon the avowal that suspensions have been made on party grounds alone, nor the threat proposed in the resolutions now before the Senate that no confirmations will be made unless the demands of that body be complied with, are sufficient to discourage or deter me from following in the way which I am convinced leads to better government for the people.

GROVER CLEVELAND

SPECIAL MESSAGE TO CONGRESS
LABOR LEGISLATION
April 22, 1886

Due to the labor disputes of 1886 President Cleveland became intensely interested in the labor problem. He then issued the first message in American History ever sent to Congress concerning labor. Since working men felt that the Government tended to favor capital and that they were suffering from the exactions of their employers, Cleveland felt that a start should be made in providing the benefits of legislation for the working class. This was to be done by setting up a permanent board for voluntary arbitration of labor disputes.

Executive Mansion, April 22, 1886

To the Senate and House of Representatives:

The Constitution imposes upon the President the duty of recommending to the consideration of Congress from time to time such measures as he shall judge necessary and expedient.

I am so deeply impressed with the importance of immediately and thoughtfully meeting the problem which recent events and a present condition have thrust upon us, involving the settlement of disputes arising between our laboring men and their employers that I am constrained to recommend to Congress legislation upon this serious and pressing subject.

Under our form of government the value of labor as an element of national prosperity should be distinctly recognized, and the welfare of the laboring man should be regarded as especially entitled to legislative care. In a country which offers to all its citizens the highest attainment of social and political distinction its workingmen can not justly or safely be considered as irrevocably consigned to the limits of a class and entitled to no attention and allowed no protest against neglect.

The laboring man, bearing in his hands an indispensable contribution to our growth and progress, may well insist, with manly courage and as a right, upon the same recognition from those who make our laws as is accorded to any other citizen having a valuable interest in charge; and his reasonable demands should be met in such a spirit of appreciation and fairness as to induce a contented and patriotic cooperation in the achievement of a grand national destiny.

While the real interests of labor are not promoted by a resort to threats and violent manifestations, and while those who, under the pretext of an advocacy of the claims of labor, wantonly attack the rights of capital and for selfish purposes or the love of disorder sow seeds of violence and discontent should neither be encouraged nor conciliated, all legislation on the subject should be calmly and deliberately undertaken, with no purpose of satisfying unreasonable demands or gaining partisan advantage.

The present condition of the relations between labor and capital is far from satisfactory. The discontent of the employed is due in a large degree to the grasping and heedless exactions of employers and the alleged discrimination in favor of capital as an object of governmental attention. It must also be conceded that the laboring men are not always careful to avoid causeless and unjustifiable disturbance.

Though the importance of a better accord between these interests is apparent, it must be borne in mind that any effort in that direction by the Federal Government must be greatly limited by constitutional restrictions. There are many grievances which legislation by Congress can not redress, and many conditions which can not only by such means be reformed.

I am satisfied, however, that something may be done under Federal authority to prevent the disturbances which so often arise from disputes between employers and the employed, and which at times seriously threaten the business interests of the country; and, in my opinion, the proper theory upon which to proceed is that of voluntary arbitration as the means of settling difficulties.

But I suggest that instead of arbitration chosen in the heat of conflicting claims, and after each dispute shall arise, for the purpose of determining the same, there be created a commission of labor, consisting of three members, who shall be regular officers of the Government, charged among other duties with the consideration and settlement, when possible, of all controversies between labor and capital.

A commission thus organized would have the advantage of being a stable body, and its members, as they gained experience, would constantly improve in their ability to deal intelligently and usefully with the questions which might be submitted to them. If arbitrators are chosen for temporary service as each case of dispute arises, experience and familiarity with much that is involved in the question will be lacking, extreme partisanship and bias will be the qualifications sought on either side, and frequent complaints of unfairness and partiality will be inevitable. The imposition upon a Federal court of a duty so foreign to the judicial function as the selection of an arbitrator in such case is at least of doubtful propriety.

The establishment by Federal authority of such a bureau would be a just and sensible recognition of the value of labor and of its right to be represented in the departments of the Government. So far as its conciliatory offices shall have relation to disturbances, which interfere with transit and commerce between the States, its existence would be justified under the provision of the Constitution which gives to Congress the power "to regulate commerce with foreign nations and among the several States;" and in the frequent disputes between the laboring men and their employers, bf less extent, and the consequences of which are confined within State limits and threaten domestic violence, the interposition of such a commission might be tendered, upon the application of the legislature or executive of a State, under the constitutional provision which requires the General Government to "protect" each of the States "against domestic violence."

If such a commission were fairly organized, the risk of a loss of popular support and sympathy resulting from a refusal to submit to so peaceful an instrumentality would constrain both parties to such disputes to invoke its interference and abide by its decisions. There would also be good reason to hope that the very existence of such an agency would invite application to it for advice and counsel, frequently resulting in the avoidance of contention and misunderstanding.

If the usefulness of such a commission is doubted because it might lack power to enforce its decisions, much encouragement is derived from the conceded good that has been accomplished by the railroad commissions which have been organized in many of the States, which, having little more than advisory power, have exerted a most salutary influence in the settlement of disputes between conflicting interests.

In July, 1884, by a law of Congress, a Bureau of Labor was established and placed in charge of a Commissioner of Labor, who is required to "collect information upon the subject of labor, its relations to capital, the hours of labor and the earnings of laboring men and women, and the means of promoting their material, social, intellectual, and moral prosperity."

The commission which I suggest could easily be ingrafted upon the bureau thus already organized by the addition of two more commissioners and by supplementing the duties now imposed upon it by such other powers and functions as would permit the commissioners to act as arbitrators when necessary between labor and capital, under such limitations and upon such occasions as should be deemed proper and useful.

Power should also be distinctly conferred upon this bureau to investigate the causes of all disputes as they occur, whether submitted for arbitration or not, so that information may always be at hand to aid legislation on the subject when necessary and desirable.

GROVER CLEVELAND

EXECUTIVE ORDER:
POLITICAL ACTIVITIES OF GOVERNMENT OFFICEHOLDERS
July 14, 1886

In this order Cleveland warned all appointed officials that they were not to use their positions as means of controlling political movements in their localities.

Executive Mansion, July 14, 1886

To the Heads of Departments in the Senate of the General Government:

I deem this is a proper time to especially warn all subordinates in the several Departments and all officeholders under the General Government against the use of their official positions in attempts to control political movements in their localities.

Officeholders are the agents of the people, not their masters. Not only is their time and labor due to the Government, but they should scrupulously avoid in their political action, as well as in the discharge of their official duty, offending by a display of obtrusive partisanship their neighbors who have relations with them as public officials.

They should also constantly remember that their party friends from whom they have received preferment have not invested them with the power of arbitrarily managing their political affairs. They have no right as officeholders to dictate the political action of their party associates or to throttle freedom of action within party lines by methods and practices which pervert every useful and justifiable purpose of party organization.

The influence of Federal officeholders should not be felt in the manipulation of political primary meetings and nominating conventions. The use by these officials of their positions to compass their selection as delegates to political conventions is indecent and unfair; and proper regard for the proprieties and requirements of official place will also prevent their assuming the active conduct of political campaigns.

Individual interest and activity in political affairs are by no means condemned. Officeholders are neither disfranchised nor forbidden the exercise of political privileges, but their privileges are not enlarged nor is their duty to party increased to pernicious activity by officeholding.

A just discrimination in this regard between the things a citizen may properly do and the purposes for which a public office should not be used is easy in the light of a correct appreciation of the relation between the people and those intrusted with official place and a consideration of the necessity under our form of government of political action free from official coercion.

You are requested to communicate the substance of these views to those for whose guidance they are intended.

Grover Cleveland

VETOES OF PENSION LEGISLATION
I.   VETO OF PENSION OF ANDREW J. HILL
May 8, 1886

Cleveland complained that too many special bills for pensions were being presented, when such cases should in fact be rare. He approved of some of these acts because of merit, although the Pensions Bureau had turned them down for lack of sufficient evidence. Others, he did not have time to study and would allow them to become law without his signature. The reason for this specific veto was the use of the wrong name.

Executive Mansion, May 8, 1886

To the House of Representatives:

I return without my approval House Bill No. 1471, entitled "An Act increasing the pension of Andrew J. Hill."

This bill doubles the pension which the person named therein has been receiving for a number of years. It appears from the report of the committee to which the bill was referred that a claim made by him for increased pension has been lately rejected by the Pension Bureau "on the ground that the claimant is now receiving a pension commensurate with the degree of disability found to exist."

The policy of frequently reversing by special enactment the decisions of the Bureau invested by law with the examination of pension claims, fully equipped for such examination, and which ought not to be suspected of any lack of liberality to our veteran soldiers, is exceedingly questionable. It may well be doubted if a committee of Congress has a better opportunity than such an agency to judge of the merits of these claims. If, however, there is any lack of power in the Pension Bureau for a full investigation, it should be supplied; if the system adopted is inadequate to do full justice to claimants, it should be corrected, and if there is a want of sympathy and consideration for the defenders of our Government the Bureau should be reorganized.

The disposition is to concede the most generous treatment to the disabled, aged, and needy among our veterans ought not to be restrained; and it must be admitted that in some cases justice and equity can not be done nor the charitable tendencies of the Government in favor of worthy objects of its care indulged under fixed rules. These conditions sometimes justify a resort to special legislation, but I am convinced that the inter-position by special enactment in the granting of pensions should be rare and exceptional. In the nature of things if this is lightly done and upon slight occasion, an invitation is offered for the presentation of claims to Congress which upon their merits could not survive the test of an exam-ination by the Pension Bureau, and whose only hope of success depends upon sympathy, often misdirected, instead of right and justice. The in-strumentality organized by law for the determination of pension claims is thus often overruled and discredited, and there is danger that in the end popular prejudice will be created against those who are worthily en-titled to the bounty of the Government.

There has lately been presented to me, on the same day, for approval, nearly 240 special bills granting and increasing pensions and restoring to the pension list the names of parties which for causes have been dropped. To aid Executive duty they were referred to the Pension Bureau for exam-ination and report. After a delay absolutely necessary they have been returned to me within a few hours of the limit constitutionally permitted for Executive action. Two hundred and thirty-two of these bills are thus classified:

Eighty-one cover cases in which favorable action by the Pension Bureau was denied by reason of the insufficiency of the testimony filed to prove the facts alleged.

These bills I have approved on the assumption that the claims were meritorious and that by the passage of the bills the Government has waived full proof of the facts.

Twenty-six of the bills cover claims rejected by the Pension Bureau be-cause the evidence produced tended to prove that the alleged disability ex-isted before the claimant's enlistment; 21 cover claims which have been denied by such Bureau because the evidence tended to show that the dis-ability, though contracted in the service, was not incurred in the line of duty; 33 cover claims which have been denied because the evidence tended to establish that the disability originated after the soldier's discharge from the Army; 47 cover claims which have been denied because the general pension laws contain no provisions under which they could be allowed, and 24 of the claims have never been presented to the Pension Bureau.

I estimate the expenditure involved in these bills at more than $35,000 annually.

Though my conception of public duty leads me to the conclusion, upon the slight examination which I have been able to give such of these bills as are not comprised on the first class above mentioned, that many of them should be disapproved, I am utterly unable to submit within the time allowed me for that purpose my objections to the same.

They will therefore become operative without my approval.

A sufficient reason for the return of the particular bill now under consideration is found in the fact that it provides that the name of Andrew J. Hill be placed upon the pension roll, while the records of the Pension Bureau, as well as a medical certificate made a part of the committee's report, disclose that the correct name of the intended beneficiary is Alfred J. Hill.

GROVER CLEVELAND

VETOES OF PENSION LEGISLATION
II.   VETO OF DEPENDENT PENSIONS BILL
February 11, 1887

The Blair bill offered a government stipend to every disabled veteran of at least three months' honorable service who was dependent for support on his own exertions, and also pensioned dependent parents of soldiers who had died in the service. Cleveland vetoed the bill because he did not believe that any of the veterans of the Civil War would want to have the pension rolls so indiscriminately expanded with no limitations or definitions of "support" and "disability."

Executive Mansion, February 11, 1887

To The House of Representatives:

I herewith return without my approval House bill No. 10457, entitled "An act for the relief of dependent parents and honorably discharged soldiers and sailors who are now disabled and dependent upon their own labor for support."

This is the first general bill that has been sanctioned by the Congress since the close of the late civil war permitting a pension to the soldiers and sailors who served in that war upon the ground of service and present disability alone, and in the entire absence of any injuries received by the casualties or incidents of such service.

While by almost constant legislation since the close of this war there has been compensation awarded for every possible injury received as a result of military service in the Union Army, and while a great number of laws passed for that purpose have been administered with great liberality and have been supplemented by numerous private acts to reach special cases, there has not until now been an avowed departure from the principle thus far adhered to respecting Union soliders, that the bounty of the Government in the way of pensions is generously bestowed when granted to those who, in this military service and in the line of military duty, have to a greater or less extent been disabled.

But it is a mistake to suppose that service pensions, such as are permitted by the second section of the bill under consideration, are new to our legislation. In 1818, thirty-five years after the close of the Revolutionary War, they were granted to the soldiers engaged in that struggle, conditional upon service until the end of the war or for a term not less than nine months, and requiring every beneficiary under the act to be one "who is, or hereafter by reason of his reduced circumstances in life shall be, in need of assistance from his country for support." Another law of a like character was passed in 1828, requiring service until the close of the Revolutionary War; and still another, passed in 1832, provided for those persons not included in the previous statute, but who served two years at some time during the war, and giving a proportionate sum to those who had served not less than six months.

A service-pension law was passed for the benefit of the soldiers of 1812 in the year 1871, fifty-six years after the close of that war, which required only sixty days' service; and another was passed in 1878, sixty-three years after the war, requiring only fourteen days' service.

The service-pension bill passed at this session of Congress, thirty-nine years after the close of the Mexican War, for the benefit of the soldiers of that war, requires either some degree of disability or dependency or that the claimant under its provisions should be 62 years of age, and in either case that he should have served sixty days or been actually engaged in a battle.

It will be seen that the bill of 1818 and the Mexican pension bill, being thus passed nearer the close of the wars in which its beneficiaries were engaged than the others—one thirty-five years and the other thirty-nine years after the termination of such wars—embraced persons who were quite advanced in age, assumed to be comparatively few in number, and whose circumstances, dependence, and disabilities were clearly defined and could be quite easily fixed.

The other laws referred to appear to have been passed at a time so remote from the military service of the persons which they embraced that their extreme age alone was deemed to supply a presumption of dependency and need. . . .

On the 1st day of July, 1886, 365,763 pensioners of all classes were upon the pension rolls, of whom 305,605 were survivors of the War of the Rebellion and their widows and dependents. For the year ending June 30, 1887, $75,000,000 have been appropriated for the payment of pensions, and the amount expended for that purpose from 1861 to July 1, 1886, is $808,624,811.51.

While annually paying out such a vast sum for pensions already granted, it is now proposed by the bill under consideration to award a service pension to the soldiers of all wars in which the United States has been engaged, including of course the War of the Rebellion, and to pay those entitled to the benefits of the act the sum of $12 per month.

So far as it relates to the soldiers of the late civil war, the bounty it affords them is given thirteen years earlier than it has been furnished the soldiers of any other war, and before a large majority of its beneficiaries have advanced in age beyond the strength and vigor of the prime of life.

It exacts only a military or naval service of three months, without any requirement of actual engagement with an enemy in battle, and without a subjection to any of the actual dangers of war.

The pension it awards is allowed to enlisted men who have not suffered the least injury, disability, loss, or damage of any kind, incurred in or in any degree referable to their military service, including those who never reached the front at all and those discharged from rendezvous at the close of the war, if discharged three months after enlistment. Under the last call of the President for troops, in December, 1864, 11,303 men were furnished who were thus discharged.

The section allowing this pension does, however, require, besides a service of three months and an honorable discharge, that those seeking the benefit of the act shall be such as "are now or may hereafter be suffering from mental or physical disability, not the result of their own vicious habits or gross carelessness, which incapacitates them for the performance of labor in such a degree as to render them unable to earn a support, and who are dependent upon their daily labor for support."

It provides further that such persons shall, upon making proof of the fact, "be placed on the list of invalid pensioners of the United States, and be entitled to receive for such total inability to procure their subsistence by daily labor $12 per month; and such pension shall commence from the date of the filing of the application in the Pension Office, upon proof that the disability then existed, and continue during the existence of the same in the degree herein provided: **Provided,** That persons who are now receiving pensions under existing laws, or whose claims are pending in the Pension Office, may, by application to the Commissioner of Pensions, in such form as he may prescribe, receive the benefit of this act."

It is manifestly of the utmost importance that statutes which, like pension laws, should be liberally administered as measures of benevolence in behalf of worthy beneficiaries should admit of no uncertainty as to their general objects and consequences.

Upon a careful consideration of the language of the section of this bill above given it seems to me to be so uncertain and liable to such conflicting construction and to be subject to such unjust and mischievous application as to alone furnish sufficient ground for disapproving the proposed legislation.

Persons seeking to obtain the pension provided by this section must be now or hereafter—

1. "Suffering from mental or physical disability."

2. Such disability must not be "the result of their own vicious habits or gross carelessness."

3. Such disability must be such as "incapacitates them for the performance of labor in such a degree as to render them unable to earn a support."

4. They must be "dependent upon their daily labor for support."

5. Upon proof of these conditions they shall "be placed on the lists of invalid pensioners of the United States, and be entitled to receive for such total inability to procure their subsistence by daily labor $12 per month."

It is not probable that the words last quoted, "such total inability to procure their subsistence by daily labor," at all qualify the conditions prescribed in the preceding language of the section. The "total inability" spoken of must be "such" inability—that is, the inability already described and constituted by the conditions already detailed in the previous parts of the section.

It thus becomes important to consider the meaning and the scope of these last-mentioned conditions.

The mental and physical disability spoken of has a distinct meaning in the practice of the Pension Bureau and includes every impairment of bodily or mental strength and vigor. For such disabilities there are now paid 131 different rates of pension, ranging from $1 to $100 per month.

This disability must not be the result of the applicant's "vicious habits or gross carelessness." Practically this provision is not important. The attempt of the Government to escape the payment of a pension on such a plea would of course in a very large majority of instances, and regardless of the merits of the case, prove a failure. There would be that strange but nearly universal willingness to help the individual as between him and the public Treasury which goes very far to insure a state of proof in favor of the claimant.

The disability of applicants must be such as to "incapacitate them for the performance of labor in such a degree as to render them unable to earn a support."

It will be observed that there is no limitation or definition of the incapacitating injury or ailment itself. It need only be such a degree of disability from any cause as renders the claimant unable to earn a support by labor. It seems to me that the "support" here mentioned as one which can not be earned is a complete and entire support, with no diminution on account of the least impairment of physical or mental condition. If it had been intended to embrace only those who by disease or injury were totally unable to labor, it would have been very easy to express that idea, instead of recognizing, as is done, a "degree" of such inability.

What is a support? Who is to determine whether a man earns it, or has it, or has it not? Is the Government to enter the homes of claimants for pension and after an examination of their surroundings and circumstances settle those questions? Shall the Government say to one man that his manner of subsistence by his earnings is a support and to another that the things his earnings furnish are not a support? Any attempt, however honest, to administer this law in such a manner would necessarily produce more unfairness and unjust discrimination and give more scope for partisan partiality, and would result in more perversion of the Government's benevolent intentions, than the execution of any statute ought to permit.

If in the effort to carry out the proposed law the degree of disability as related to earnings be considered for the purpose of discovering if in any way it curtails the support which the applicant, if entirely sound, would earn, and to which he is entitled, we enter the broad field long occupied by the Pension Bureau, and we recognize as the only difference between the proposed legislation and previous laws passed for the benefit of the surviving soldiers of the Civil War the incurrence in one case of disabilities in military service and in the other disabilities existing, but in no way connected with or resulting from such service.

It must be borne in mind that in no case is there any grading of this proposed pension. Under the operation of the rule first suggested, if there is a lack in any degree, great or small, of the ability to earn such a support as the Government determines the claimant should have, and, by the application of the rule secondly suggested, if there is a reduction in any degree of the support which he might earn if sound, he is entitled to a pension of $12. . . .

As to the meaning of the section of the bill under consideration there appears to have been quite a difference of opinion among its advocates in the Congress. The chairman of the Committee on Pensions in the House of Representatives, who reported the bill, declared that there was in it no provision for pensioning anyone who has a less disability than a total inability to labor, and that it was a charity measure. The chairman of the Committee on Pensions in the Senate, having charge of the bill in that body, dissented from the construction of the bill announced in the House of Representatives, and declared that it not only embraced all soldiers totally disabled, but, in his judgment, all who are disabled to any considerable extent; and such a construction was substantially given to the bill by another distinguished Senator, who, as a former Secretary of the Interior had imposed upon him the duty of executing pension laws and determining their intent and meaning.

Another condition required of claimants under this act is that they shall be "dependent upon their daily labor for support."

This language, which may be said to assume that there exists within the reach of the persons mentioned "labor," or the ability in some degree to work, is more aptly used in a statute describing those not wholly deprived of this ability than in one which deals with those utterly unable to work.

I am of the opinion that it may fairly be contended that under the provisions of this section any soldier whose faculties of mind or body have become impaired by accident, disease, or age, irrespective of his service in the Army as a cause, and who by his labor only is left incapable of gaining the fair support he might with unimpaired powers have provided for himself, and who is not so well endowed with this world's goods as to live without work, may claim to participate in its bounty; that it is not required that he should be without property, but only that labor should be necessary to his support in some degree; nor is it required that he should be now receiving support from others.

Believing this to be the proper interpretation of the bill, I can not but remember that the soldiers of our Civil War in their pay and bounty received such compensation for military service as has never been received by soldiers before since mankind first went to war; that never before on behalf of any soldiery have so many and such generous laws been passed to relieve against the incidents of war; that statutes have been passed giving them a preference in all public employments; that the really needy and homeless Union soldiers of the rebellion have been to a large extent provided for at soldiers' homes, instituted and supported by the Government, where they are maintained together, free from the sense of degradation which attaches to the usual support of charity; and that never before in the history of the country has it been proposed to render Government aid toward the support of any of its soldiers based alone upon a military service so recent, and where age and circumstances appeared so little to demand such aid.

Hitherto such relief has been granted to surviving soldiers few in number, venerable in age, after a long lapse of time since their military service, and as a parting benefaction tendered by a grateful people.

I can not believe that the vast peaceful army of Union soldiers, who, having contentedly resumed their places in the ordinary avocations of life, cherish as sacred the memory of patriotic service, or who, having been disabled by the casualties of war, justly regard the present pension roll on which appear their names as a roll of honor, desire at this time and in the present exigency to be confounded with those who through such a bill as this are willing to be objects of simple charity and to gain a place upon the pension roll through alleged dependence.

Recent personal observation and experience constrain me to refer to another result which will inevitably follow the passage of this bill. It is sad, but nevertheless true, that already in the matter of procuring pensions there exists a widespread disregard of truth and good faith, stimulated by those who as agents undertake to establish claims for pensions heedlessly entered upon by the expectant beneficiary, and encouraged, or at least not condemned, by those unwilling to obstruct a neighbor's plans.

In the execution of this proposed law under any interpretation a wide field of inquiry should be opened for the establishment of facts largely within the knowledge of the claimants alone, and there can be no doubt that the race after the pensions offered by this bill would not only stimlate weakness and pretended incapacity for labor, but put a further premium on dishonesty and mendacity. . . .

If none should be pensioned under this bill except those utterly unable to work, I am satisfied that the cost stated in the estimate referred to would be many times multiplied, and with a constant increase from year to year; and if those partially unable to earn their support should be admitted to the privileges of this bill, the probable increase of expense would be almost appalling.

I think it may be said that at the close of the War of the Rebellion every Northern State and a great majority of Northern counties and cities were burdened with taxation on account of the large bounties paid our soldiers; and the bonded debt thereby created still constitutes a large item in the account of the taxgatherer against the people. Federal taxation, no less borne by the people than that directly levied upon their property, is still maintained at the rate made necessary by the exigencies of war. If this bill should become a law, with its tremendous addition to our pension obligation, I am thoroughly convinced that further efforts to reduce the Federal revenue and restore some part of it to our people will, and perhaps should, be seriously questioned.

It has constantly been a cause of pride and congratulation to the American citizen that his country is not put to the charge of maintaining a large standing army in time of peace. Yet we are now living under a war tax which has been tolerated in peaceful times to meet the obligations incurred in war. But for years past, in all parts of the country, the demand for the reduction of the burdens of taxation upon our labor and production has increased in volume and urgency.

I am not willing to approve a measure presenting the objections to which this bill is subject, and which, moreover, will have the effect of disappointing the expectation of the people and their desire and hope for relief from war taxation in time of peace.

In my last annual message the following language was used:

> Every patriotic heart responds to a tender consideration for those who, having served their country long and well, are reduced to destitution and dependence, not as an incident of their service, but with advancing age or through sickness or misfortune. We are all tempted by the contemplation of such a condition to supply relief, and are often impatient of the limitations of public duty. Yielding to no one in the desire to indulge this feeling of consideration, I can not rid myself of the conviction that if these ex-soldiers are to be relieved they and their cause are entitled to the benefit of an enactment under which relief may be claimed as a right, and that such relief should be granted under the

sanction of law, not in evasion of it; nor should such worthy objects of care, all equally entitled, be remitted to the unequal operation of sympathy or the tender mercies of social and political influence, with their unjust discriminations.

I do not think that the objects, the conditions, and the limitations thus suggested are contained in the bill under consideration.

I adhere to the sentiments thus heretofore expressed. But the evil threatened by this bill is, in my opinion, such that, charged with a great responsibility in behalf of the people, I can not do otherwise than to bring to the consideration of this measure my best efforts of thought and judgment and perform my constitutional duty in relation thereto, regardless of all consequences except such as appear to me to be related to the best and highest interests of the country.

GROVER CLEVELAND

VETO OF TEXAS SEED BILL
February 16, 1887

In his veto of the Texas Seed Bill which would have provided seed grain to those counties in Texas which had suffered from a drought Cleveland indicated his dislike of paternalism in government. He maintained that the Federal Government had a limited mission, and that such attempts on the part of Congress to extend its activities were wrong because the "Government should not support the people." He believed that paternal care on the part of the Government would weaken the national character.

Executive Mansion, February 16, 1887

To the House of Representatives:

I return without my approval House bill No. 10203, entitled "An act to enable the Commissioner of Agriculture to make a special distribution of seeds in the drought-stricken counties of Texas, and making an appropriation therefor."

It is represented that a long-continued and extensive drought has existed in certain portions of the State of Texas, resulting in a failure of crops and consequent distress and destitution.

Though there has been some difference in statements concerning the extent of the people's needs in the localities thus affected, there seems to be no doubt that there has existed a condition calling for relief; and I am willing to believe that, notwithstanding the aid already furnished, a donation of seed grain to the farmers located in this region, to enable them to put in new crops, would serve to avert a continuance or return of an unfortunate blight.

And yet I feel obliged to withhold my approval of the plan, as proposed by this bill, to indulge a benevolent and charitable sentiment through the appropriation of public funds for that purpose.

I can find no warrant for such an appropriation in the Constitution, and I do not believe that the power and duty of the General Government ought to be extended to the relief of individual suffering which is in no manner properly related to the public service or benefit. A prevalent tendency to disregard the limited mission of this power and duty should, I think, be steadfastly resisted, to the end that the lesson should be constantly enforced that though the people support the Government the Government should not support the people.

The friendliness and charity of our countrymen can always be relied upon to relieve their fellow-citizens in misfortune. This has been repeatedly and quite lately demonstrated. Federal aid in such cases encourages the expectation of paternal care on the part of the Government and weakens the sturdiness of our national character, while it prevents the indulgence among our people of that kindly sentiment and conduct which strengthens the bonds of a common brotherhood.

It is within my personal knowledge that individual aid has to some extent already been extended to the sufferers mentioned in this bill. The failure of the proposed appropriation of $10,000 additional to meet their remaining wants will not necessarily result in continued distress if the emergency is fully made known to the people of the country.

It is here suggested that the Commissioner of Agriculture is annually directed to expend a large sum of money for the purchase, propagation, and distribution of seeds and other things of this description, two-thirds of which are, upon the request of Senators, Representatives, and Delegates in Congress, supplied to them for distribution among their constituents.

The appropriation of the current year for this purpose is $100,000, and it will probably be no less in the appropriation for the ensuing year. I understand that a large quantity of grain is furnished for such distribution, and it is supposed that this free apportionment among their neighbors is a privilege which may be waived by our Senators and Representatives.

If sufficient of them should request the Commissioner of Agriculture to send their shares of the grain thus allowed them to the suffering farmers of Texas, they might be enabled to sow their crops, the constituents for whom in theory this grain is intended could well bear the temporary deprivation, and the donors would experience the satisfaction attending deeds of charity.

GROVER CLEVELAND

THIRD ANNUAL MESSAGE
December 6, 1887

In this unique message Cleveland dealt with one item: the tariff. As a result of discussion throughout the country, it was inevitable that a lowering of the tariff should be proposed. The message was a sweeping arraignment of a tariff system in which protection had been raised to great extremes. It was to arouse a hue and cry throughout the nation and stimulated the "Great Tariff Debate" of 1888.

WASHINGTON, December 6, 1887

To the Congress of the United States:

You are confronted at the threshold of your legislative duties with a condition of the national finances which imperatively demands immediate and careful consideration.

The amount of money annually exacted, through the operation of present laws, from the industries and necessities of the people largely exceeds the sum necessary to meet the expenses of the Government.

When we consider that the theory of our institutions guarantees to every citizen the full enjoyment of all the fruits of his industry and enterprise, with only such deduction as may be his share toward the careful and economical maintenance of the Government which protects him, it is plain that the exaction of more than this is indefensible extortion and a culpable betrayal of American fairness and justice. This wrong inflicted upon those who bear the burden of national taxation, like other wrongs, multiplies a brood of evil consequences. The public Treasury, which should only exist as a conduit conveying the people's tribute to its legitimate objects of expenditure, becomes a hoarding place for money needlessly withdrawn from trade and the people's use, thus crippling our national energies, suspending our country's development, preventing investment in productive enterprise, threatening financial disturbance, and inviting schemes of public plunder.

This condition of our Treasury is not altogether new, and it has more than once of late been submitted to the people's representatives in the Congress, who alone can apply a remedy. And yet the situation still continues, with aggravated incidents, more than ever presaging financial convulsion and widespread disaster.

It will not do to neglect this situation because its dangers are not now palpably imminent and apparent. They exist none the less certainly, and await the unforeseen and unexpected occasion when suddenly they will be precipitated upon us.

On the 30th day of June, 1885, the excess of revenues over public expenditures, after complying with the annual requirement of the sinking-fund act, was $17,859,735.84; during the year ended June 30, 1886, such excess amounted to $49,405,545.20, and during the year ended June 30, 1887, it reached the sum of $55,567,849.54.

The annual contributions to the sinking fund during the three years above specified, amounting in the aggregate to $138,058,320.94, and deducted from the surplus as stated, were made by calling in for that purpose outstanding 3 per cent bonds of the Government. During the six months prior to June 30, 1887, the surplus revenue had grown so large by repeated accumulations, and it was feared the withdrawal of this great sum of money needed by the people would so affect the business of the country, that the sum of $79,864,100 of such surplus was applied to the payment of the principal and interest of the 3 per cent bonds still outstanding, and which were then payable at the option of the Government. The precarious condition of financial affairs among the people still needing relief, immediately after the 30th day of June, 1887, the remainder of the 3 per cent bonds then outstanding, amounting with principal and interest to the sum of $18,877,500, were called in and applied to the sinking-fund contribution for the current fiscal year. Notwithstanding these operations of the Treasury Department, representations of distress in business circles not only continued, but increased, and absolute peril seemed at hand. In these circumstances the contribution to the sinking fund for the current fiscal year was at once completed by the expenditure of $27,684,283.55 in the purchase of Government bonds not yet due bearing 4 and 4-1/2 per cent interest, the premium paid thereon averaging about 24 per cent for the former and 8 per cent for the latter. In addition to this, the interest accruing during the current year upon the outstanding bonded indebtedness of the Government was to some extent anticipated, and banks selected as depositories of public money were permitted to somewhat increase their deposits.

While the expedients thus employed to release to the people the money lying idle in the Treasury served to avert immediate danger, our surplus revenues have continued to accumulate, the excess for the present year amounting on the 1st day of December to $55,258,701.19, and estimated to reach the sum of $113,000,000 on the 30th of June next, at which date it is expected that this sum, added to prior accumulations, will swell the surplus in the Treasury to $140,000,000.

There seems to be no assurance that, with such a withdrawal from use of the people's circulating medium, our business community may not in the near future be subjected to the same distress which was quite lately produced from the same cause. And while the functions of our National Treasury should be few and simple, and while its best condition would be reached, I believe, by its entire disconnection with private business interests, yet when, by a perversion of its purposes, it idly holds money uselessly subtracted from the channels of trade, there seems to be reason for the claim that some legitimate means should be devised by the Government to restore in an emergency, without waste or extravagance, such money to its place among the people.

If such an emergency arises, there now exists no clear and undoubted executive power of relief. Heretofore the redemption of 3 per cent bonds, which were payable at the option of the Government, has afforded a means for the disbursement of the excess of our revenues; but these bonds have all been retired, and there are no bonds outstanding the payment of which we have a right to insist upon. The contribution to the sinking fund which furnishes the occasion for expenditure in the purchase of bonds has been already made for the current year, so that there is no outlet in that direction.

In the present state of legislation the only pretense of any existing executive power to restore at this time any part of our surplus revenues to the people by its expenditure consists in the supposition that the Secretary of the Treasury may enter the market and purchase the bonds of the Government not yet due, at a rate of premium to be agreed upon. The only provision of law from which such a power could be derived is found in an appropriation bill passed a number of years ago, and it is subject to the suspicion that it was intended as temporary and limited in its application, instead of conferring a continuing discretion and authority. No condition ought to exist which would justify the grant of power to a single official, upon his judgment of its necessity, to withhold from or release to the business of the people, in an unusual manner, money held in the Treasury, and thus affect at his will the financial situation of the country; and if it is deemed wise to lodge in the Secretary of the Treasury the authority in the present juncture to purchase bonds, it should be plainly vested, and provided, as far as possible, with such checks and limitations as will define this official's right and discretion and at the same time relieve him from undue responsibility.

In considering the question of purchasing bonds as a means of restoring to circulation the surplus money accumulating in the Treasury, it should be borne in mind that premiums must of course be paid upon such purchase, that there may be a large part of these bonds held as investments which can not be purchased at any price, and that combinations among holders who are willing to sell may unreasonably enhance the cost of such bonds to the Government.

It has been suggested that the present bonded debt might be refunded at a less rate of interest and the difference between the old and new security paid in cash, thus finding use for the surplus in the Treasury. The success of this plan, it is apparent, must depend upon the volition of the holders of the present bonds; and it is not entirely certain that the inducement which must be offered them would result in more financial benefit to the Government than the purchase of bonds, while the latter proposition would reduce the principal of the debt by actual payment instead of extending it.

The proposition to deposit the money held by the Government in banks throughout the country for use by the people is, it seems to me, exceedingly objectionable in principle, as establishing too close a relationship between the operations of the Government Treasury and the business of the country and too extensive a commingling of their money, thus fostering an unnatural reliance in private business upon public funds. If this scheme should be adopted, it should only be done as a temporary expedient to meet an urgent necessity. Legislative and executive effort should generally be in the opposite direction, and should have a tendency to divorce, as much and as fast as can be safely done, the Treasury Department from private enterprise.

Of course it is not expected that unnecessary and extragant appropriations will be made for the purpose of avoiding the accumulation of an excess of revenue. Such expenditure, besides the demoralization of all just conceptions of public duty which it entails, stimulates a habit of reckless improvidence not in the least consistent with the mission of our people or the high and beneficent purposes of our Government. . . .

Our scheme of taxation, by means of which this needless surplus is taken from the people and put into the public Treasury, consists of a tariff or duty levied upon importations from abroad and internal-revenue taxes levied upon the consumption of tobacco and spirituous and malt liquors. It must be conceded that none of the things subjected to internal-revenue taxation are, strictly speaking, necessaries. There appears to be no just complaint of this taxation by the consumers of these articles, and there seems to be nothing so well able to bear the burden without hardship to any portion of the people.

But our present tariff laws, the vicious, inequitable, and illogical source of unnecessary taxation, ought to be at once revised and amended. These laws, as their primary and plain effect, raise the price to consumers of all articles imported and subject to duty by precisely the sum paid for such duties. Thus the amount of the duty measures the tax paid by those who purchase for use these imported articles. Many of these things, however, are raised or manufactured in our own country, and the duties now levied upon foreign goods and products are called protection to these home manufactures, because they render it possible for those of our people who are manufacturers to make these taxed articles and sell them for a price equal to that demanded for the imported goods that have paid customs duty. So it happens that while comparatively a few use the imported articles, millions of our people, who never used and never saw any of the foreign products, purchase and use things of the same kind made in this country, and pay therefor nearly or quite the same enhanced price which the duty adds to the imported articles. Those who buy imports pay the duty charged thereon into the public Treasury, but the great majority of our citizens, who buy domestic articles of the same class, pay a sum at least approximately equal to this duty to the home manufacturer. This reference to the operation of our tariff laws is not made by way of instruction, but in order that we may be constantly reminded of the manner in which they impose a burden upon those who consume domestic products as well as those who consume imported articles, and thus create a tax upon all our people.

It is not proposed to entirely relieve the country of this taxation. It must be extensively continued as the source of the Government's income; and in a readjustment of our tariff the interests of American labor engaged in manufacture should be carefully considered, as well as the preservation of our manufacturers. It may be called protection or by any other name, but relief from the hardships and dangers of our present tariff laws should be devised with especial precaution against imperiling the existence of our manufacturing interests. But this existence should not mean a condition which, without regard to the public welfare or a national exigency, must always insure the realization of immense profits instead of moderately profitable returns. As the volume and diversity of our national activities increase, new recruits are added to those who desire a continuation of the advantages which they conceive the present system of tariff taxation directly affords them. So stubbornly have all efforts to reform the present condition been resisted by those of our fellow-citizens thus engaged that they can hardly complain of the suspicion, entertained to a certain extent, that there exists an organized combination all along the line to maintain their advantage.

We are in the midst of centennial celebrations, and with becoming pride we rejoice in American skill and ingenuity, in American energy and enterprise, and in the wonderful natural advantages and resources developed by a century's national growth. Yet when an attempt is made to justify a scheme which permits a tax to be laid upon every consumer in the land for the benefit of our manufacturers, quite beyond a reasonable demand for governmental regard, it suits the purposes of advocacy to call our manufactures infant industries still needing the highest and greatest degree of favor and fostering care that can be wrung from Federal legislation.

It is also said that the increase in the price of domestic manufactures resulting from the present tariff is necessary in order that higher wages may be paid to our workingmen employed in manufactories than are paid for what is called the pauper labor of Europe. All will acknowledge the force of an argument which involves the welfare and liberal compensation of our laboring people. Our labor is honorable in the eyes of every American citizen; and as it lies at the foundation of our development and progress, it is entitled, without affectation or hypocrisy, to the utmost regard. The standard of our laborers' life should not be measured by that of any other country less favored, and they are entitled to their full share of all our advantages. . . .

The reduction of taxation demanded should be so measured as not to necessitate or justify either the loss of employment by the workingman or the lessening of his wages; and the profits still remaining to the manufacturer after a necessary readjustment should furnish no excuse for the sacrifice of the interests of his employees, either in their opportunity to work or in the diminution of their compensation. Nor can the worker in manufactures fail to understand that while a high tariff is claimed to be necessary to allow the payment of remunerative wages, it certainly results in a very large increase in the price of nearly all sorts of manufactures, which, in almost countless forms, he needs for the use of himself and his family. He receives at the desk of his employer his wages, and perhaps before he reaches his home is obliged, in a purchase for family use of an article which embraces his own labor, to return in the payment of the increase in price which the tariff permits the hard-earned compensation of many days of toil.

The farmer and the agriculturist, who manufacture nothing, but who pay the increased price which the tariff imposes upon every agricultural implement, upon all he wears, and upon all he uses and owns, except the increase of his flocks and herds and such things as his husbandry produces from the soil, is invited to aid in maintaining the present situation; and he is told that a high duty on imported wool is necessary for the benefit of those who have sheep to shear, in order that the price of their wool may be increased. They, of course, are not reminded that the farmer who has no sheep is by this scheme obliged, in his purchases of clothing and woolen goods, to pay a tribute to his fellow-farmer as well as to the manufacturer and merchant, nor is any mention made of the fact that the sheep owners themselves and their households must wear clothing and use other articles manufactured from the wool they sell at tariff prices, and thus as consumers must return their share of this increased price to the tradesman. . . .

In speaking of the increased cost to the consumer of our home manufactures resulting from a duty laid upon imported articles of the same description, the fact is not overlooked that competition among our domestic producers sometimes has the effect of keeping the price of their products below the highest limit allowed by such duty. But it is notorious that this competition is too often strangled by combinations quite prevalent at this time, and frequently called trusts, which have for their object the regulation of the supply and price of commodities made and sold by members of the combination. The people can hardly hope for any consideration in the operation of these selfish schemes.

If, however, in the absence of such combination, a healthy and free competition reduces the price of any particular dutiable article of home production below the limit which it might otherwise reach under our tariff laws, and if with such reduced price its manufacture continues to thrive, it is entirely evident that one thing has been discovered which should be carefully scrutinized in an effort to reduce taxation.

The necessity of combination to maintain the price of any commodity to the tariff point furnishes proof that someone is willing to accept lower prices for such commodity and that such prices are remunerative; and lower prices produced by competition prove the same thing. Thus where either of these conditions exists a case would seem to be presented for an easy reduction of taxation.

The considerations which have been presented touching our tariff laws are intended only to enforce an earnest recommendation that the surplus revenues of the Government be prevented by the reduction of our customs duties, and at the same time to emphasize a suggestion that in accomplishing this purpose we may discharge a double duty to our people by granting to them a measure of relief from tariff taxation in quarters where it is most needed and from sources where it can be most fairly and justly accorded.

Nor can the presentation made of such considerations be with any degree of fairness regarded as evidence of unfriendliness toward our manufacturing interests or of any lack of appreciation of their value and importance.

These interests constitute a leading and most substantial element of our national greatness and furnish the proud proof of our country's progress. But if in the emergency that presses upon us our manufacturers are asked to surrender something for the public good and to avert disaster, their patriotism, as well as a grateful recognition of advantages already afforded, should lead them to willing cooperation. No demand is made that they shall forego all the benefits of governmental regard; but they can not fail to be admonished of their duty, as well as their enlightened self-interest and safety, when they are reminded of the fact that financial panic and collapse, to which the present condition tends, afford no greater shelter or protection to our manufactures than to other important enterprises. Opportunity for safe, careful, and deliberate reform is now offered; and none of us should be unmindful of a time when an abused and irritated people, heedless of those who have resisted timely and reasonable relief, may insist upon a radical and sweeping rectification of their wrongs.

The difficulty attending a wise and fair revision of our tariff laws is not underestimated. It will require on the part of the Congress great labor and care, and especially a broad and national contemplation of the subject and a patriotic disregard of such local and selfish claims as are unreasonable and reckless of the welfare of the entire country.

Under our present laws more than 4,000 articles are subject to duty. Many of these do not in any way compete with our own manufactures, and many are hardly worth attention as subjects of revenue. A considerable reduction can be made in the aggregate by adding them to the free list. The taxation of luxuries presents no features of hardship; but the necessaries of life used and consumed by all the people, the duty upon which adds to the cost of living in every home, should be greatly cheapened.

The radical reduction of the duties imposed upon raw material used in manufactures, or its free importation, is of course an important factor in any effort to reduce the price of these necessaries. It would not only relieve them from the increased cost caused by the tariff on such material, but the manufactured product being thus cheapened that part of the tariff now laid upon such product, as a compensation to our manufacturers for the present price of raw material, could be accordingly modified. Such reduction or free importation would serve besides to largely reduce the revenue. It is not apparent how such a change can have any injurious effect upon our manufacturers. On the contrary, it would appear to give them a better chance in foreign markets with the manufacturers of other countries, who cheapen their wares by free material. Thus our people might have the opportunity of extending their sales beyond the limits of home consumption, saving them from the depression, interruption in business, and loss caused by a glutted domestic market and affording their employees more certain and steady labor, with its resulting quiet and contentment.

The question thus imperatively presented for solution should be approached in a spirit higher than partisanship and considered in the light of that regard for patriotic duty which should characterize the action of those intrusted with the weal of a confiding people. But the obligation to declared party policy and principle is not wanting to urge prompt and effective action. Both of the great political parties now represented in the Government have by repeated and authoritative declarations condemned the condition of our laws which permit the collection from the people of unnecessary revenue, and have in the most solemn manner promised its correction; and neither as citizens nor partisans are our countrymen in a mood to condone the deliberate violation of these pledges.

Our progress toward a wise conclusion will not be improved by dwelling upon the theories of protection and free trade. This savors too much of bandying epithets. It is a **condition** which confronts us, not a theory. Relief from this condition may involve a slight reduction of the advantages which we award our home productions, but the entire withdrawal of such advantages should not be contemplated. The question of free trade is absolutely irrelevant, and the persistent claim made in certain quarters that all the efforts to relieve the people from unjust and unnecessary taxation are schemes of so-called free traders is mischievous and far removed from any consideration for the public good.

The simple and plain duty which we owe the people is to reduce taxation to the necessary expenses of an economical operation of the Government and to restore to the business of the country the money which we hold in the Treasury through the perversion of governmental powers. These things can and should be done with safety to all our industries, without danger to the opportunity for remunerative labor which our workingmen need, and with benefit to them and all our people by cheapening their means of subsistence and increasing the measure of their comforts. . . .

GROVER CLEVELAND

SPECIAL MESSAGE TO CONGRESS:
RAILROAD INVESTIGATION
January 17, 1888

President Cleveland submitted with this message the majority and minority reports of the commissioners appointed by the Act of March 3, 1887, to investigate the affairs of those railroads which had received aid from the Federal Government. The two reports could not agree on the method of settling the indebtedness of the railways to the Government. Cleveland urged that Congress study the two reports and decide on the best method of settlement for the benefit of the American people.

EXECUTIVE MANSION, **January 17, 1888**

To the Senate and House of Representatives:

On the 3d day of March last an act was passed authorizing the appointment of three commissioners who should investigate the affairs of such railroads as have received aid from the United States Government. Among other things, the contemplated investigation included a history of the construction of these roads, their relations and indebtedness to the Government, and the question whether in the interest of the United States any extension of the time for the performance of the obligations of said roads to the Government should be granted; and if so, the said commissioners were directed to submit a scheme for such extension. . . .

The commissioners have, however, been unable to agree upon the manner in which these railroads should be treated respecting their indebtedness to the United States, or to unite upon the plan best calculated to secure the payment of such indebtedness.

This disagreement has resulted in the preparation of two reports, both of which are herewith submitted to the Congress.

These reports exhibit such transaction and schemes connected with the construction of the aided roads and their management, and suggest the invention of such devices on the part of those having them in charge, for the apparent purpose of defeating any chance for the Government's reimbursement, that any adjustment or plan of settlement should be predicated upon the substantial interests of the Government rather than any forbearance or generosity deserved by the companies.

The wide publication which has already been given to the substance of the commissioners' reports obviates the necessity of detailing in this communication the facts found upon the investigation.

The majority report, while condemning the methods adopted by those who formerly had charge of the Union Pacific Railroad, declares that since its present management was inaugurated, in 1884, its affairs have been fairly and prudently conducted, and that the present administration "has devoted itself honestly and intelligently to the herculean task of rescuing the Union Pacific Railway from the insolvency which seriously threatened it at the inception of its work;" that it "has devoted itself, by rigid economy, by intelligent management, and by an application of every dollar of the earning capacity of the system to its improvement and betterment, to place that company on a sound and enduring financial foundation."

The condition of the present management of the Union Pacific Company has an important bearing upon its ability to comply with the terms of any settlement of its indebtedness which may be offered by the Government.

The majority of the commission are in favor of an extension of the time for the payment of the Government indebtedness of these companies, upon certain conditions; but the chairman of the commission, presenting the minority report, recommends, both upon principle and policy, the institution of proceedings for the forfeiture of the charters of the corporations and the winding up of their affairs.

I have been furnished with a statement or argument in defense of the transactions connected with the construction of the Central Pacific road and its branch lines, from which it may not be amiss to quote for the purpose of showing how some of the operations of the directors of such road, strongly condemned by the commissioners, are defended by the directors themselves. After speaking of a contract for the construction of one of these branch lines by a corporation called the Contract and Finance Company, owned by certain directors of the Central Pacific Railroad, this language is used:

It may be said of this contract, as of many others that were let to the different construction companies in which the directors of the Central Pacific have been stockholders, that they built the road with the moneys furnished by themselves and had the road for their outlay. In other words, they paid to the construction company the bonds and stock of the railroad so constructed, and waited until such time as they could develop sufficient business on the road built to induce the public to buy the bonds or the stock. If the country through which the railroad ran developed sufficient business, then the project was a success; if it did not, then the operation was a loss. These gentlemen took all the responsibility; any loss occurring was necessarily theirs, and of right the profit belonged to them.

But it is said that they violated a well-known rule of equity in dealing with themselves; that they were trustees, and that they were representing both sides of the contract.

The answer is that they did not find anybody else to deal with. They could not find anyone who would take the chances of building a road through what was then an almost uninhabited country and accept the bonds and stock of the road in payment. And when it is said that they were trustees, if they did occupy such relation it was merely technical, for they represented only their own interests on both sides, there being no one else concerned in the transaction. They became the incorporators of the company that was to build the road subscribed for its stock, and were the only subscribers; therefore it is difficult to see how anyone was wronged by their action. The rule of equity invoked, which has its origin in the injunction "No man can serve two masters," certainly did not apply to them, because they were acting in their own interests and were not charged with the duty of caring for others' rights, there being no other persons interested in the subject-matter.

In view of this statement and the facts developed in the commissioners' reports, it seems proper to recall the grants and benefits derived from the General Government by both the Union and Central Pacific companies for the purpose of aiding the construction of their roads.

By an act passed in 1862 it was provided that there should be advanced to said companies by the United States, to aid in such construction, the bonds of the Government amounting to $16,000 for every mile constructed, as often as a section of 40 miles of said roads should be built; that there should also be granted to said companies, upon the completion of every said section of 40 miles of road, five entire sections of public land for each mile so built; that the entire charges earned by said roads on account of transportation and service for the Government should be applied to the reimbursement of the bonds advanced by the United States and the interest thereon, and that to secure the repayment of the bonds so advanced, and interest, the issue and delivery to said companies of said bonds should constitute a first mortgage on the whole line of their roads and on their rolling stock, fixtures, and property of every kind and description.

The liberal donations, advances, and privileges provided for in this law were granted by the General Government for the purpose of securing the construction of these roads, which would complete the connection between our eastern and western coasts; and they were based upon a consideration of the public benefits which would accrue to the entire country from such consideration.

But the projectors of these roads were not content, and the sentiment which then seemed to pervade the Congress had not reached the limit of its generosity. Two years after the passage of this law it was supplemented and amended in various important particulars in favor of these companies by an act which provided, among other things, that the bonds, at the rate already specified, should be delivered upon the completion of sections of 20 miles in length instead of 40; that the lands to be conveyed to said companies on the completion of each section of said road should be ten sections per mile instead of five; that only half of the charges for transportation and service due from time to time from the United States should be retained and applied to the advances made to said companies by the Government, thus obliging immediate payment to its debtor of the other half of said charges, and that the lien of the United States to secure the reimbursement of the amount advanced to said companies in bonds, which lien was declared by the law of 1862 to constitute a first mortgage upon all the property of said companies, should become a junior lien and be subordinated to a mortgage which the companies were by the amendatory act authorized to execute to secure bonds which they might from time to time issue in sums not exceeding the amount of the United States bonds which should be advanced to them.

The immense advantages to the companies of this amendatory act are apparent; and in these days we may well wonder that even the anticipated public importance of the construction of these roads induced what must now appear to be a rather reckless and unguarded appropriation of the public funds and the public domain.

Under the operation of these laws the principal of the bonds which have been advanced is $64,023,512, . . . the interest to November 1, 1887, is calculated to be $76,024,206.58, making an aggregate at the date named of $140,047,718.58. The interest calculated to the maturity of the bonds added to the principal produces an aggregate of $178,884,759.50. Against these amounts there has been repaid by the companies the sum of $30,955,039.61.

It is almost needless to state that the companies have availed themselves to the utmost extent of the permission given them to issue their bonds and to mortgage their property to secure the payment of the same, by an incumbrance having preference to the Government's lien and precisely equal to it in amount.

It will be seen that there was available for the building of each mile of these roads $16,000 of United States bonds, due in thirty years, with 6 per cent interest; $16,000 in bonds of the companies, secured by a first mortgage on all their property, and ten sections of Government land, to say nothing of the stock of the companies.

When the relations created between the Government and these companies by the legislation referred to is considered, it is astonishing that the claim should be made that the directors of these roads owed no duty except to themselves in their construction; that they need regard no interests but their own, and that they were justified in contracting with themselves and making such bargains as resulted in conveying to their pockets all the assets of the companies. As a lienor the Government was vitally interested in the amount of the mortgage to which its security had been subordinated, and it had the right to insist that none of the bonds secured by this prior mortgage should be issued fraudulently or for the purpose of division among these stockholders without consideration.

The doctrine of complete independence on the part of the directors of these companies and their freedom from any obligation to care for other interests than their own in the construction of these roads seems to have developed the natural consequences of its application, portrayed as follows in the majority report of the commissioners:

The result is that those who have controlled and directed the construction and development of these companies have become possessed of their surplus assets through issues of bonds, stocks, and payment of dividends voted by themselves, while the great creditor, the United States, finds itself substantially without adequate security for the repayment of its loands.

The laws enacted in aid of these roads, while they illustrated a profuse liberality and a generous surrender of the Government's advantages, which it is hoped experience has corrected, were nevertheless passed upon the theory that the roads should be constructed according to the common rules of business, fairness, and duty, and that their value and their ability to pay their debts should not be impaired by unfair manipulations; and when the Government subordinated its lien to another it was in the expectation that the prior lien would represent in its amount only such bonds as should be necessarily issued by the companies for the construction of their roads at fair prices, agreed upon in an honest way between real and substantial parties. For the purpose of saving or improving the security afforded by its junior lien the Government should have the right now to purge this paramount lien of all that is fraudulent, fictitious, or unconscionable. If the transfer to innocent hands of bonds of this character secured by such first mortgage prevents their cancellation, it might be well to seek a remedy against those who issued and transferred them. If legislation is needed to secure such a remedy, the Congress can readily supply it.

I desire to call attention also to the fact that if all that was to be done on the part of the Government to fully vest in these companies the grants and advantages contemplated by the acts passed in their interest has not yet been perfected, and if the failure of such companies to perform in good faith their part of the contract justifies such a course, the power rests with the Congress to withhold further performance on the part of the Government. If donated lands are not yet granted to these companies, and if their violation of contract and of duty are such as in justice and morals forfeit their rights to such lands, Congressional action should intervene to prevent further consummation. Executive power must be exercised according to existing laws, and Executive discretion is probably not broad enought to reach such difficulties. . . .

It is quite time that the troublesome complications surrounding this entire subject, which has been transmitted to us as a legacy from former days, should be adjusted and settled.

No one, I think, expects that these railroad companies will be able to pay their immense indebtedness to the Government at its maturity.

Any proceeding or arrangement that would result now, or at any other time, in putting these roads, or any portion of them, in the possession and control of the Government is, in my opinion, to be rejected, certainly as long as there is the least chance for indemnification through any other means.

I suppose we are hardly justified in indulging the irritation and indignation naturally arising from a contemplation of malfeasance to such an extent as to lead to the useless destruction of these roads or loss of the advances made by the Government. I believe that our efforts should be in a more practical direction, and should tend, with no condonation of wrongdoing, to the collection by the Government, on behalf of the people, of the public money now in jeopardy.

While the plan presented by a majority of the commission appears to be well devised and gives at least partial promise of the results sought, the fact will not escape attention that its success depends upon its acceptance by the companies and their ability to perform its conditions after acceptance. It is exceedingly important that any adjustment now made should be final and effective. These considerations suggest the possibility that the remedy proposed in the majority report might well be applied to a part only of these aided railroad companies.

The settlement and determination of the questions involved are peculiarly within the province of the Congress. The subject has been made quite a familiar one by Congressional discussion. This is now supplemented in a valuable manner by the facts presented in the reports herewith submitted.

The public interest urges prompt and efficient action.

GROVER CLEVELAND

SPECIAL MESSAGE TO CONGRESS:
Civil Service Commission Report
July 23, 1888

In this fourth report of the United States Civil Service Commission, Cleveland not only discussed the technical advances of the previous year but also presented a general summary of the problems and work involved in civil service reform. The selection below deals with this general summary.

Executive Mansion, July 23, 1888

To the Congress of the United States:

. . . The path of civil-service reform has not at all times been pleasant nor easy. The scope and purpose of the reform have been much misapprehended; and this has not only given rise to strong opposition, but has led to its invocation by its friends to compass objects not in the least related to it. Thus partisans of the patronage system have naturally condemned it. Those who do not understand its meaning either mistrust it or, when disappointed because in its present stage it is not applied to every real or imaginary ill, accuse those charged with its enforcement with faithfulness to civil-service reform. Its importance has frequently been underestimated, and the support of good men has thus been lost by their lack of interest in its success. Besides all these difficulties, those responsible for the administration of the Government in its executive branches have been and still are often annoyed and irritated by the disloyalty to the service and the insolence of employees who remain in place as the beneficiaries and the relics and reminders of the vicious system of appointment which civil-service reform was intended to displace.

And yet these are but the incidents of an advance movement which is radical and far-reaching. The people are, notwithstanding, to be congratulated upon the progress which has been made and upon the firm, practical, and sensible foundation upon which this reform now rests.

With a continuation of the intelligent fidelity which has hitherto characterized the work of the Commission; with a continuation and increase of the favor and liberality which have lately been evinced by the Congress in the proper equipment of the Commission for its work; with a firm but conservative and reasonable support of the reform by all its friends and with the disappearance of opposition which must inevitably follow its better understanding, the execution of the civil-service law can not fail to ultimately answer the hopes in which it had its origin.

SECOND INAUGURAL ADDRESS
March 4, 1893

In this address to the nation Cleveland reiterated his desire for civil-service reform. He also indicated a need to dissolve illegal business and manufacturing combinations; to protect the Indians, and to revise taxation.

MY FELLOW-CITIZENS: In obedience to the mandate of my country-men I am about to dedicate myself to their service under the sanction of a solemn oath. Deeply moved by the expression of confidence and personal attachment which has called me to this service, I am sure my gratitude can make no better return than the pledge I now give before God and these witnesses of unreserved and complete devotion to the interests and welfare of those who have honored me.

I deem it fitting on this occasion, while indicating the opinions I hold concerning public questions of present importance, to also briefly refer to the existence of certain conditions and tendencies among our people which seem to menace the integrity and usefulness of their Government.

While every American citizen must contemplate with the utmost pride and enthusiasm the growth and expansion of our country, the sufficiency of our institutions to stand against the rudest shocks of violence, the wonderful thrift and enterprise of our people, and the demonstrated superiority of our free government, it behooves us to constantly watch for every symptom of insidious infirmity that threatens our national vigor.

The strong man who in the confidence of sturdy health courts the sternest activities of life and rejoices in the hardihood of constant labor may still have lurking near his vitals the unheeded disease that dooms him to sudden collapse.

It can not be doubted that our stupendous achievements as a people and our country's robust strength have given rise to heedlessness of those laws governing our national health which we can no more evade than human life can escape the laws of God and nature.

Manifestly nothing is more vital to our supremacy as a nation and to the beneficent purposes of our Government than a sound and stable currency. Its exposure to degradation should at once arouse to activity the most enlightened statemanship, and the danger of depreciation in the purchasing power of the wages paid to toil should furnish the strongest incentive to prompt and conservative precaution.

In dealing with our present embarrassing situation as related to this subject we will be wise if we temper our confidence and faith in our national strength and resources with the frank concession that even these will not permit us to defy with impunity the inexorable laws of finance and trade. At the same time, in our efforts to adjust differences of opinion we should be free from intolerance or passion, and our judgments should be unmoved by alluring phrases and unvexed by selfish interests.

I am confident that such an approach to the subject will result in prudent and effective remedial legislation. In the meantime, so far as the executive branch of the Government can intervene, none of the powers with which it is invested will be withheld when their exercise is deemed necessary to maintain our national credit or avert financial disaster.

Closely related to the exaggerated confidence in our country's greatness which tends to a disregard of the rules of national safety, another danger confronts us not less serious. I refer to the prevalence of a popular disposition to expect from the operation of the Government especial and direct individual advantages.

The verdict of our voters which condemned the injustice of maintaining protection for protection's sake enjoins upon the people's servants the duty of exposing and destroying the brood of kindred evils which are the unwholesome progeny of paternalism. This is the bane of republican institutions and the constant peril of our government by the people. It degrades to the purposes of wily craft the plan of rule our fathers established and bequeathed to us as an object of our love and veneration. It perverts the patriotic sentiments of our countrymen and tempts them to pitiful calculation of the sordid gain to be derived from their Government's maintenance. It undermines the self-reliance of our people and substitutes in its place dependence upon governmental favoritism. It stifles the spirit of true Americanism and stupefies every ennobling trait of American citizenship.

The lessons of paternalism ought to be unlearned and the better lesson taught that while the people should patriotically and cheerfully support their Government its functions do not include the support of the people.

The acceptance of this principle leads to a refusal of bounties and subsidies, which burden the labor and thrift of a portion of our citizens to aid ill-advised or languishing enterprises in which they have no concern. It leads also to a challenge of wild and reckless pension expenditure, which overleaps the bounds of grateful recognition of patriotic service and prostitutes to vicious uses the people's prompt and generous impulse to aid those disabled in their country's defense.

Every thoughtful American must realize the importance of checking at its beginning any tendency in public or private station to regard frugality and economy as virtues which we may safely outgrow. The toleration of this idea results in the waste of the people's money by their chosen servants and encourages prodigality and extravagance in the home life of our countrymen.

Under our scheme of government the waste of public money is a crime against the citizen, and the contempt of our people for economy and frugality in their personal affairs deplorably saps the strength and sturdiness of our national character.

It is a plain dictate of honesty and good government that public expenditures should be limited by public necessity, and that this should be measured by the rules of strict economy; and it is equally clear that frugality among the people is the best guaranty of a contented and strong support of free institutions.

One mode of the misappropriation of public funds is avoided when appointments to office, instead of being the rewards of partisan activity, are awarded to those whose efficiency promises a fair return of work for the compensation paid to them. To secure the fitness and competency of appointees to office and remove from political action the demoralizing madness for spoils, civil-service reform has found a place in our public policy and laws. The benefits already gained through this instrumentality and the further usefulness it promises entitle it to the hearty support and encouragement of all who desire to see our public service well performed or who hope for the elevation of political sentiment and the purification of political methods.

The existence of immense aggregations of kindred enterprises and combinations of business interests formed for the purpose of limiting production and fixing prices is inconsistent with the fair field which ought to be open to every independent activity. Legitimate strife in business should not be superseded by an enforced concession to the demands of combinations that have the power to destroy, nor should the people to be served lose the benefit of cheapness which usually results from wholesome competition. These aggregations and combinations frequently constitute conspiracies against the interests of the people, and in all their phases they are unnatural and opposed to our American sense of fairness. To the extent that they can be reached and restrained by Federal power the General Government should relieve our citizens from their interference and exactions.

Loyalty to the principles upon which our Government rests positively demands that the equality before the law which it guarantees to every citizen should be justly and in good faith conceded in all parts of the land. The enjoyment of this right follows the badge of citizenship wherever found, and, unimpaired by race or color, it appeals for recognition to American manliness and fairness.

Our relations with the Indians located within our border impose upon us responsibilities we can not esacpe. Humanity and consistency require us to treat them with forbearance and in our dealings with them to honestly and considerately regard their rights and interests. Every effort should be made to lead them, through the paths of civilization and education, to self-supporting and independent citizenship. In the meantime, as the nation's wards, they should be promptly defended against the cupidity of designing men and shielded from every influence or temptation that retards their advancement.

The people of tne United States have decreed that on this day the control of their Government in its legislative and executive branches shall be given to a political party pledged in the most positive terms to the accomplishment of tariff reform. They have thus determined in favor of a more just and equitable system of Federal taxation. The agents they have chosen to carry out their purposes are bound by their promises not less than by the command of their masters to devote themselves unremittingly to this service.

While there should be no surrender of principle, our task must be undertaken wisely and without heedless vindictiveness. Our mission is not punishment, but the rectification of wrong. If in lifting burdens from the daily life of our people we reduce inordinate and unequal advantages too long enjoyed, this is but a necessary incident of our return to right and justice. If we exact from unwilling minds acquiescence in the theory of an honest distribution of the fund of the governmental beneficence treasured up for all, we but insist upon a principle which underlies our free institutions. 'When we tear aside the delusions and misconceptions which have blinded our countrymen to their condition under vicious tariff laws, we but snow them how far they have been led away from the paths of contentment and prosperity. When we proclaim that the necessity for revenue to support the Government furnishes the only justification for taxing the people, we announce a truth so plain that its denial would seem to indicate the extent to which judgment may be influenced by familiarity with perversions of the taxing power. And when we seek to reinstate the self-confidence and business enterprise of our citizens by discrediting an abject dependence upon governmental favor, we strive to stimulate those elements of American character which support the hope of American achievement.

Anxiety for the redemption of the pledges which my party has made and solicitude for the complete justification of the trust the people have reposed in us constrain me to remind those with whom I am to cooperate that we can succeed in doing the work which has been especially set before us only by the most sincere, harmonious, and disinterested effort. Even if insuperable obstacles and opposition prevent the consummation of our task, we shall hardly be excused; and if failure can be traced to our fault or neglect we may be sure the people will hold us to a swift and exacting accountability.

The oath I now take to preserve, protect, and defend the Constitution of the United States not only impressively defines the great responsibility I assume, but suggests obedience to constitutional commands as the rule by which my official conduct must be guided. I shall to the best of my ability and within my sphere of duty preserve the Constitution by loyally protecting every grant of Federal power it contains, by defending all its restraints when attacked by impatience and restlessness, and by enforcing its limitations and reservations in favor of the States and the people.

Fully impressed with the gravity of the duties that confront me and mindful of my weakness, I should be appalled if it were my lot to bear unaided the responsibilities which await me. I am, however, saved from discouragement when I remember that I shall have the support and the counsel and cooperation of wise and patriotic men who will stand at my side in Cabinet places or will represent the people in their legislative halls.

I find also much comfort in remembering that my countrymen are just and generous and in the assurance that they will not condemn those who by sincere devotion to their service deserve their forbearance and approval.

Above all, I know there is a Supreme Being who rules the affairs of men and whose goodness and mercy have always followed the American people, and I know He will not turn from us now if we humbly and reverently seek His powerful aid.

MARCH 4, 1893

EXECUTIVE ORDER:
Interviews with the President
May 8, 1893

In this statement Cleveland indicated the great drain on his time which personal interviews with office seekers and their sponsors, as well as constituents of Congressmen, were taking. He excluded these types of meetings, from his schedule.

Executive Mansion, May 8, 1893

It has become apparent after two months' experience that the rules heretofore promulgated regulating interviews with the President have wholly failed in their operation. The time which under these rules was set apart for the reception of Senators and Representatives has been almost entirely spent in listening to applications for office, which have been bewildering in volume, perplexing and exhausting in their iteration and impossible of remembrance.

A due regard for public duty, which must be neglected if present conditions continue, and an observance of the limitation placed upon human endurance oblige me to decline from and after this date all personal interviews with those seeking appointments to office, except as I on my own motion may especially invite them. The same considerations make it impossible for me to receive those who merely desire to pay their respects except on the days and during the hours especially designed for that purpose.

I earnestly request Senators and Representatives to aid me in securing for them uninterrupted interviews by declining to introduce their constituents and friends when visiting the Executive Mansion during the hours designated for their reception. Applicants for office will only prejudice their prospects by repeated importunity and by remaining in Washington to await results.

GROVER CLEVELAND

SPECIAL SESSION MESSAGE:
Silver Currency Problem
August 8, 1893

This message, completed by Attorney General Richard Olney because of Cleveland's incapacity, indicated the dangers of continuing the policy of silver coinage as outlined in the Sherman Silver Purchase Act of July 14, 1890. The President indicated the rapidly shrinking gold reserve in the Treasury, arguing for the need to guarantee the people "a sound and stable currency." Cleveland therefore urged the repeal of the provision of the Act of 1890 authorizing the purchase of silver bullion.

Executive Mansion, August 8, 1893

To the Congress of the United States:

The existence of an alarming and extraordinary business situation involving the welfare and prosperity of all our people, has constrained me to call together in extra session the people's representatives in Congress, to the end that through a wise and patriotic exercise of the legislative duty, with which they solely are charged, present evils may be mitigated and dangers threatening the future may be averted.

Our unfortunate financial plight is not the result of untoward events nor of conditions related to our natural resources, nor is it traceable to any of the afflictions which frequently check national growth and prosperity. With plenteous crops, with abundant promise of remunerative production and manufacture, with unusual invitation to safe investment, and with satisfactory assurance to business enterprise, suddenly financial distrust and fear have sprung up on every side. Numerous moneyed institutions have suspended because abundant assets were not immediately available to meet the demands of frightened depositors. Surviving corporations and individuals are content to keep in hand the money they are usually anxious to loan, and those engaged in legitimate business are surprised to find that the securities they offer for loans, though heretofore satisfactory, are no longer accepted. Values supposed to be fixed are fast becoming conjectural, and loss and failure have invaded every branch of business.

I believe these things are principally chargeable to Congressional legislation touching the purchase and coinage of silver by the General Government.

This legislation is embodied in a statute passed on the 14th day of July, 1890, which was the culmination of much agitation on the subject involved, and which may be considered a truce, after a long struggle, between the advocates of free silver coinage and those intending to be more conservative.

Undoubtedly the monthly purchases by the Government of 4,500,000 ounces of silver, enforced under that statute, were regarded by those interested in silver production as a certain guaranty of its increase in price. The result, however, has been entirely different, for immediately following a spasmodic and slight rise the price of silver began to fall after the passage of the act, and has since reached the lowest point ever known. This disappointing result has led to renewed and persistent effort in the direction of free silver coinage.

Meanwhile not only are the evil effects of the operation of the present law constantly accumulating, but the result to which its execution must inevitably lead is becoming palpable to all who give the least heed to financial subjects.

This law provides that in payment for the 4,500,000 ounces of silver bullion which the Secretary of the Treasury is commanded to purchase monthly there shall be issued Treasury notes redeemable on demand in gold or silver coin, at the discretion of the Secretary of the Treasury, and that said notes may be reissued. It is, however, declared in the act to be "the established policy of the United States to maintain the two metals on a parity with each other upon the present legal ratio or such ratio as may be provided by law." This declaration so controls the action of the Secretary of the Treasury as to prevent his exercising the discretion nominally vested in him if by such action the parity between gold and silver may be disturbed. Manifestly a refusal by the Secretary to pay these Treasury notes in gold if demanded would necessarily result in their discredit and depreciation as obligations payable only in silver, and would destroy the parity between the two metals by establishing a discrimination in favor of gold.

Up to the 15th day of July, 1893, these notes had been issued in payment of silver-bullion purchases to the amount of more than $147,000,-000. While all but a very small quantity of this bullion remains uncoined and without usefulness in the Treasury, many of the notes given in its purchase have been paid in gold. This is illustrated by the statement that between the 1st day of May, 1892, and the 15th day of July, 1893, the notes of this kind issues in payment for silver bullion amounted to a little more than $54,000,000, and that during the same period about $9,000,000 were paid by the Treasury in gold for the redemption of such notes.

The policy necessarily adopted of paying these notes in gold has not spared the gold reserve of $100,000,000 long ago set aside by the Government for the redemption of other notes, for this fund has already been subjected to the payment of new obligations amounting to about $150,000,000 on account of silver purchases, and has as a consequence for the first time since its creation been encroached upon.

We have thus made the depletion of our gold easy and have tempted other and more appreciative nations to add it to their stock. That the opportunity we have offered has not been neglected is shown by the large amounts of gold which have been recently drawn from our Treasury and exported to increase the financial strength of foreign nations. The excess of exports of gold over imports for the year ending June 30, 1893, amounted to more than $87,500,000.

Between the 1st day of July, 1890, and the 15th day of July, 1893, the gold coin and bullion in our Treasury decreased more than $132,000,-000, while during the same period the silver coin and bullion in the Treasury increased more than $147,000,000. Unless Government bonds are to be constantly issued and sold to replenish our exhausted gold, only to be again exhausted, it is apparent that the operation of the silver-purchase law now in force leads in the direction of the entire substitution of silver for the gold in the Government Treasury, and that this must be followed by the payment of all Government obligations in depreciated silver.

At this stage gold and silver must part company and the Government must fail in its established policy to maintain the two metals on a parity with each other. Given over to the exclusive uses of a currency greatly depreciated according to the standard of the commercial world, we could no longer claim a place among nations of the first class, nor could our Government claim a performance of its obligation, so far as such an obligation has been imposed upon it, to provide for the use of the people the best and safest money.

If, as many of its friends claim, silver ought to occupy a larger place in our currency and the currency of the world through general international cooperation and agreement, it is obvious that the United States will not be in a position to gain a hearing in favor of such an arrangement so long as we are willing to continue our attempt to accomplish the result singlehanded.

The knowledge in business circles among our own people that our Government can not make its fiat equivalent to intrinsic value nor keep inferior money on a parity with superior money by its own independent efforts has resulted in such a lack of confidence at home in the stability of currency values that capital refuses its aid to new enterprises, while millions are actually withdrawn from the channels of trade and commerce to become idle and unproductive in the hands of timid owners. Foreign investors, equally alert, not only decline to purchase American securities, but make haste to sacrifice those which they already have.

It does not meet the situation to say that apprehension in regard to the future of our finances is groundless and that there is no reason for lack of confidence in the purposes or power of the Government in the premises. The very existence of this apprehension and lack of confidence, however caused, is a menace which ought not for a moment to be disregarded. Possibly, if the undertaking we have in hand were the maintenance of a specific known quality of silver at a parity with gold, our ability to do so might be estimated and gauged, and perhaps, in view of our unparalleled growth and resources, might be favorably passed upon. But when our avowed endeavor is to maintain such parity in regard to an amount of silver increasing at the rate of $50,000,000 yearly, with no fixed termination to such increase, it can hardly be said that a problem is presented whose solution is free from doubt.

The people of the United States are entitled to a sound and stable currency and to money recognized as such on every exchange and in every market of the world. Their Government has no right to injure them by financial experiments opposed to the policy and practice of other civilized states, nor is it justified in permitting an exaggerated and unreasonable reliance on our national strength and ability to jeopardize the soundness of the people's money.

This matter rises above the plane of party politics. It vitally concerns every business and calling and enters every household in the land. There is one important aspect of the subject which especially should never be overlooked. At times like the present, when the evils of unsound finance threaten us, the speculator may anticipate a harvest gathered from the misfortune of others, the capitalist may protect himself by hoarding or may even profit in the fluctuations of values; but the wage earner—the first to be injured by a depreciated currency and the last to receive the benefit of its correction—is practically defenseless. He relies for work upon the ventures of confident and contented capital. This failing him, his condition is without alleviation, for he can neither prey on the misfortunes of others nor hoard his labor. One of the greatest statesmen our country has known, speaking more than fifty years ago, when a derangement of the currency has caused commercial distress, said:

> The very man of all others who has the deepest interest in a
> sound currency and who suffers most by mischevious legislation

in money matters is the man who earns his daily bread by his daily toil.

These words are as pertinent now as on the day they were uttered, and ought to impressively remind us that a failure in the discharge of our duty at this time must especially injure those of our countrymen who labor, and who because of their number and condition are entitled to the most watchful care of their Government.

It is of the utmost importance that such relief as Congress can afford in the existing situation be afforded at once. The maxim "He gives twice who gives quickly" is directly applicable. It may be true that the embarassments from which the business of the country is suffering arise as much from evils apprehended as from those actually existing. We may hope, too, that calm counsels will prevail, and that neither the capitalists nor the wage earners will give way to unreasoning panic and sacrifice their property or interests under the influence of exaggerated fears. Nevertheless, every day's delay in removing one of the plain and principal causes of the present state of things enlarges the mischief already done and increases the responsibility of the Government for its existence. Whatever else the people have a right to expect from Congress, they may certainly demand that legislation condemned by the ordeal of three years' disastrous experience shall be removed from the statute books as soon as their representatives can legitimately deal with it.

It was my purpose to summon Congress in special session early in the coming September, that we might enter promptly upon the work of tariff reform, which the true interests of the country clearly demand, which so large a majority of the people, as shown by their suffrages, desire and expect and to the accomplishment of which every effort of the present Administration is pledged. But while tariff reform has lost nothing of its immediate and permanent importance and must in the near future engage the attention of Congress, it has seemed to me that the financial condition of the country should at once and before all other subjects be considered by your honorable body.

I earnestly recommend the prompt repeal of the provisions of the act passed July 14, 1890, authorizing the purchase of silver bullion, and that other legislative action and the ability of the Government to fulfill its pecuniary obligations in money universally recognized by all civilized countries.

GROVER CLEVELAND

SPECIAL MESSAGE TO CONGRESS:
Hawaiian Situation
December 18, 1893

Cleveland had withdrawn the Treaty of Annexation between the United States and the Provisional Government of the Hawaiian Islands on March 9, 1893. Subsequently he ordered an investigation by Turner H. Blount whose report is the basis of this message. Cleveland indicated the illegality of the actions of the American Minister and the American troops in Hawaii in regard to the revolution. As a result of the study Cleveland was convinced that the time was inopportune for the annexation of Hawaii.

EXECUTIVE MANSION
Washington, December 18, 1893

To the Senate and House of Representatives:

In my recent annual message to the Congress I briefly referred to our relations with Hawaii and expressed the intention of transmitting further information on the subject when additional advices permitted.

Though I am not able now to report a definite change in the actual situation, I am convinced that the difficulties lately created both here and in Hawaii, and now standing in the way of a solution through Executive action of the problem presented, render it proper and expedient that the matter should be referred to the broader authority and discretion of Congress, with a full explanation of the endeavor thus far made to deal with the emergency and a statement of the considerations which have governed my action.

I suppose that right and justice should determine the path to be followed in treating this subject. If national honesty is to be disregarded and a desire for territorial extension or dissatisfaction with a form of government not our own ought to regulate our conduct, I have entirely misapprehended the mission and character of our Government and the behavior which the conscience of our people demands of their public servants.

When the present Administration entered upon its duties, the Senate had under consideration a treaty providing for the annexation of the Hawaiian Islands to the territory of the United States. Surely under our Constitution and laws the enlargement of our limits is a manifestation of the highest attribute of sovereignty, and if entered upon as an Executive act all things relating to the transaction should be clear and free from suspicion. Additional importance attached to this particular treaty of annexation because it contemplated a departure from unbroken American tradition in providing for the addition to our territory of islands of the sea more than 2,000 miles removed from our nearest coast.

These considerations might not of themselves call for interference with the completion of a treaty entered upon by a previous Administration, but it appeared from the documents accompanying the treaty when submitted to the Senate that the ownership of Hawaii was tendered to us by a Provisional Government set up to succeed the constitutional ruler of the islands, who had been dethroned, and it did not appear that such Provisional Government had the sanction of either popular revolution or suffrage. Two other remarkable features of the transaction naturally attracted attention. One was the extraordinary haste, not to say precipitancy, characterizing all the transactions connected with the treaty. It appeared that a so-called committee of safety, ostensibly the source of the revolt against the constitutional Government of Hawaii, was organized on Saturday, the 14th day of January; that on Monday, the 16th, the United States forces were landed at Honolulu from a naval vessel lying in its harbor; that on the 17th the scheme of a Provisional Government was perfected, and a proclamation naming its officers was on the same day prepared and read at the Government building; that immediately thereupon the United States minister recognized the Provisional Government thus created; that two days afterwards, on the 19th day of January, commissioners representing such Government sailed for this country in a steamer especially chartered for the occasion, arriving in San Francisco on the 28th day of January and in Washington on the 3d day of February; that on the next day they had their first interview with the Secretary of State, and another on the 11th, when the treaty of annexation was practically agreed upon, and that on the 14th it was formally concluded and on the 15th transmitted to the Senate. Thus between the initiation of the scheme for a Provisional Government in Hawaii, on the 14th day of January, and the submission to the Senate of the treaty of annexation concluded with such Government the entire interval was thirty-two days, fifteen of which were spent by the Hawaiian commissioners in their journey to Washington.

In the next place, upon the face of the papers submitted with the treaty it clearly appeared that there was open and undetermined an issue of fact of the most vital importance. The message of the President accompanying the treaty declared that "the overthrow of the monarchy was not in any way promoted by this Government," and in a letter to the President from the Secretary of State, also submitted to the Senate with the treaty, the following passage occurs:

At the time the Provisional Government took possession of the Government buildings no troops or officers of the United States were present or took any part whatever in the proceedings. No public recognition was accorded to the Provisional Government by the United States minister until after the Queen's abdication and when they were in effective possession of the Government buildings, the archives, the treasury, the barracks, the police station, and all the potention machinery of the Government.

But a protest also accompanied said treaty, signed by the Queen and her ministers at the time she made way for the Provisional Government, which explicitly stated that she yielded to the superior force of the United States, whose minister had caused United States troops to be landed at Honolulu and declared that he would support such Provisional Government.

The truth or falsity of this protest was surely of the first importance. If true, nothing but the concealment of its truth could induce our Government to negotiate with the semblance of a government thus created, nor could a treaty resulting from the acts stated in the protest have been knowingly deemed worthy of consideration by the Senate. Yet the truth or falsity of the protest had not been investigated.

I conceived it to be my duty, therefore, to withdraw the treaty from the Senate for examination, and meanwhile to cause an accurate, full, and impartial investigation to be made of the facts attending the subversion of the constitutional Government of Hawaii and the installment in its place of the Provisional Government. I selected for the work of investigation the Hon. James H. Blount, of Georgia, whose service of eighteen years as a member of the House of Representatives and whose experience as chairman of the Committee of Foreign Affairs in that body, and his consequent familiarity with international topics, joined with his high character and honorable reputation, seemed to render him peculiarly fitted for the duties intrusted to him. His report detailing his action under the instructions given to him and the conclusions derived from his investigation accompany this message.

These conclusions do not rest for their acceptance entirely upon Mr. Blount's honesty and ability as a man, nor upon his acumen and impartiality as an investigator. They are accompanied by the evidence upon which they are based, which evidence is also herewith transmitted, and from which it seems to me no other deductions could possibly be reached than those arrived at by the commissioner.

The report, with its accompanying proofs and such other evidence as is now before the Congress or is herewith submitted, justifies, in my opinion, the statement that when the President was led to submit the treaty to the Senate with the declaration that "the overthrow of the monarchy was not in any way promoted by this Government," and when the Senate was induced to receive and discuss it on that basis, both President and Senate were misled.

The attempt will not be made in this communication to touch upon all the facts which throw light upon the progress and consummation of this scheme of annexation. A very brief and imperfect reference to the facts and evidence at hand will exhibit its character and the incidents in which it had its birth.

It is unnecessary to set forth the reasons which in January, 1893, led a considerable proportion of American and other foreign merchants and traders residing at Honolulu to favor the annexation of Hawaii to the United States. It is sufficient to note the fact and to observe that the project was one which was zealously promoted by the minister representing the United States in that country. He evidently had an ardent desire that it should become a fact accomplished by his agency and during his ministry, and was not inconveniently scrupulous as to the means employed to that end. On the 19th day of November, 1892, nearly two months before the first overt act tending toward the subversion of the Hawaiian Government and the attempted transfer of Hawaiian territory to the United States, he addressed a long letter to the Secretary of State, in which the case for annexation was elaborately argued on moral, political, and economical grounds. He refers to the loss to the Hawaiian sugar interests from the operation of the McKinley bill and the tendency to still further depreciation of sugar property unless some positive measure of relief is granted. He strongly inveighs against the existing Hawaiian Government and emphatically declares for annexation. He says:

In truth, the monarchy here is an absurd anachronism. It has nothing on which it logically or legitimately stands. The feudal basis on which it once stood no longer existing, the monarchy now is only an impediment to good government—an obstruction to the prosperity and progress of the islands.

He further says:

As a Crown colony of Great Britain or a Territory of the United States the government modifications could be made readily and good administration of the law secured. Destiny and the vast future interests of the United States in the Pacific clearly indicate who at no distant day must be responsible for the government of these islands. Under a Territorial government they could be as easily governed as any of the existing territories of the United States. * * * Hawaii has reached the parting of the ways. She must now take the road which leads to Asia, or the other, which outlets her in America, gives her an American civilization, and binds her to the care of American destiny.

He also declares:

One to two courses seems to me absolutely necessary to be followed—either bold and vigorous measures for annexation or a "customs union," an ocean cable from the California coast to Honolulu, Pearl Harbor perpetually ceded to the United States, with an implied but not expressly stipulated American protectorate over the islands. I believe the former to be the better, that which will prove much the more advantageous to the islands and the cheapest and least embarrassing in the end to the United States. If it was wise for the United States, through Secretary Marcy, thirty-eight years ago, to offer to expend $100,000 to secure a treaty of annexation, it certainly can not be chimerical or unwise to expend $100,000 to secure annexation in the near future. To-day the United States has five times the wealth she possessed in 1854, and the reasons now existing for annexation are much stronger than they were then. I can not refrain from expressing the opinion with emphasis that the golden hour is near at hand.

These declarations certainly show a disposition and condition of mind which may be usefully recalled when interpreting the significance of the minister's conceded acts or when considering the probabilities of such conduct on his part as may not be admitted.

In this view it seems proper to also quote from a letter written by the minister to the Secretary of State on the 8th day of March, 1892, nearly a year prior to the first step taken toward annexation. After stating the possibility that the existing Government of Hawaii might be overturned by an orderly and peaceful revolution, Minister Stevens writes as follows:

Ordinarily, in like circumstances, the rule seems to be to limit the landing and movement of United States forces in foreign waters and dominion exclusively to the protection of the United States legation and of the lives and property of American citizens; but as the relations of the United States to Hawaii are exceptional, and in former years the United States officials here took somewhat exceptional action in circumstances of disorder, I desire to know how far the present minister and naval commander may deviate from established international rules and precedents in the contingencies indicated in the first part of this dispatch.

To a minister of this temper, full of zeal for annexation, there seemed to arise in January, 1893, the precise opportunity for which he was watchfully waiting—an opportunity which by timely "deviation from established international rules and precedents" might be improved to successfully accomplish the great object in view; and we are quite prepared for the exultant enthusiasm with which, in a letter to the State Department dated February 1, 1893, he declares:

The Hawaiian pear is now fully ripe, and this is the golden hour for the United States to pluck it.

As a further illustration of the activity of this diplomatic representative, attention is called to the fact that on the day the above letter was written, apparently unable longer to restrain his ardor, he issued a proclamation whereby, "in the name of the United States," he assumed the protection of the Hawaiian Islands and declared that said action was "taken pending and subject to negotiations at Washington." Of course this assumption of a protectorate was promptly disavowed by our Government, but the American flag remained over the Government building at Honolulu and the forces remained on guard until April, and after Mr. Blount's arrival on the scene, when both were removed.

A brief statement of the occurrences that led to the subversion of the constitutional Government of Hawaii in the interests of annexation to the United States will exhibit the true complexion of that transaction.

On Saturday, January 14, 1893, the Queen of Hawaii, who had been contemplating the proclamation of a new constitution, had, in deference to the wishes and remonstrances of her cabinet, renounced the project for the present at least. Taking this relinquished purpose as a basis of action, citizens of Honolulu numbering from fifty to one hundred, mostly resident aliens, met in a private office and selected a so-called committee of safety, composed of thirteen persons, seven of whom were foreign subjects, and consisted of five Americans, one Englishman, and one German. This committee, though its designs were not revealed, had in view nothing less than annexation to the United States, and between Saturday, the 14th, and the following Monday, the 16th of January—though exactly what action was taken may not be clearly disclosed—they were certainly in communication with the United States minister. On Monday morning the Queen and her cabinet made public proclamation, with a notice which was specially served upon the representatives of all foreign governments, that any changes in the constitution would be sought only in the methods provided by that instrument. Nevertheless, at the call and under the auspices of the committee of safety, a mass meeting of citizens was held on that day to protest against the Queen's alleged illegal and unlawful proceedings and purposes. Even at this meeting the committee of safety continued to disguise their real purpose and contented themselves with procuring the passage of a resolution denouncing the Queen and empowering the committee to devise ways and means "to secure the permanent maintenance of law and order and the protection of life, liberty, and property in Hawaii." This meeting adjourned between 3 and 4 o'clock in the afternoon. On the same day, and immediately after such adjournment, the committee, unwilling to take further steps without the cooperation of the United States minister, addressed him a note representing that the public safety was menaced and that lives and property were in danger, and concluded as follows:

We are unable to protect ourselves without aid, and therefore pray for the protection of the United States forces.

Whatever may be thought of the other contents of this note, the absolute truth of this latter statement is incontestable. When the note was written and delivered the committee, so far as it appears, had neither a man nor a gun at their command, and after its delivery they became so panic-stricken at their position that they sent some of their number to interview the minister and request him not to land the United States forces till the next morning. But he replied that the troops had been ordered and whether the committee were ready or not the landing should take place. And so it happened that on the 16th day of January, 1893, between 4 and 5 o'clock in the afternoon, a detachment of marines from the United States steamer **Boston**, with two pieces of artillery, landed at Honolulu. The men, upward of 160 in all, were supplied with double cartridge belts filled with ammunition and with haversacks and canteens, and were accompanied by a hospital corps with stretchers and medical supplies.

This military demonstration upon the soil of Honolulu was of itself an act of war, unless made either with the consent of the Government of Hawaii or for the **bona fide** purpose of protecting the imperiled lives and property of citizens of the United States. But there is no pretense of any such consent on the part of the Government of the Queen, which at that time was undisputed and was both the **de facto** and the **de jure** Government. In point of fact the existing Government, instead of requesting the presence of an armed force, protested against it. There is as little basis for the pretense that such forces were landed for the security of American life and property. If so, they would have been stationed in the vicinity of such property and so as to protect it, instead of at a distance and so as to command the Hawaiian Government building and palace. Admiral Skerrett, the officer in command of our naval force on the Pacific station, has frankly stated that in his opinion the location of the troops was inadvisable if they were landed for the protection of American citizens, whose residences and places of business, as well as the legation and consulate, were in a distant part of the city; but the location selected was a wise one if the forces were landed for the purpose of supporting the Provisional Government. If any peril to life and property calling for any such martial array had existed, Great Britain and other foreign powers interested would not have been behind the United States in activity to protect their citizens. But they made no sign in that direction. When these armed men were landed the city of Honolulu was in its customary orderly and peaceful condition. There was no symptom of riot or disturbance in any quarter. Men, women, and children were about the streets as usual, and nothing varied the ordinary routine or disturbed the ordinary tranquility except the landing of the **Boston's** marines and their march through the town to the quarters assigned them. Indeed, the fact that after having called for the landing of the United States forces on the plea of danger to life and property the committee of safety themselves requested the minister to postpone action exposed the untruthfulness of their representations of present peril to life and property. The peril they saw was an anticipation growing out of guilty intentions on their part and something which, though not then existing, they knew would certainly follow their attempt to overthrow the Government of the Queen without the aid of the United States forces.

Thus it appears that Hawaii was taken possession of by the United States forces without the consent or wish of the Government of the islands, or of anybody else so far as shown except the United States minister. Therefore the military occupation of Honolulu by the United States on the day mentioned was wholly without justification, either as an occupation by consent or as an occupation necessitated by dangers threatening American life and property. It must be accounted for in some other way and on some other ground, and its real motive and purpose are neither obscure nor far to seek.

The United States forces being now on the scene and favorably stationed, the committee proceeded to carry out their original scheme. They met the next morning, Tuesday, the 17th, perfected the plan of temporary government, and fixed upon its principal officers, ten of whom were drawn from the thirteen members of the committee of safety. Between 1 and 2 o'clock, by squads and by different routes to avoid notice, and having first taken the precaution of ascertaining whether there was anyone there to oppose them, they proceeded to the Government building to proclaim the new Government. No sign of opposition was manifest, and thereupon an American citizen began to read the proclamation from the steps of the Government building, almost entirely without auditors. It is said that before the reading was finished quite a concourse of persons, variously estimated at from 50 to 100, some armed and some unarmed, gathered about the committee to give them aid and confidence. This statement is not important, since the one controlling factor in the whole affair was unquestionably the United States marines, who, drawn up under arms and with artillery in readiness only 76 yards distant, dominated the situation.

The Provisional Government thus proclaimed was by the terms of the proclamation "to exist until terms of union with the United States had been negotiated and agreed upon." The United States minister, pursuant to prior agreement, recognized this Government within an hour after the reading of the proclamation, and before 5 o'clock, in answer to an inquiry on behalf of the Queen and her cabinet, announced that he had done so.

When our minister recognized the Provisional Government, the only basis upon which it rested was the fact that the committee of safety had in the manner above stated declared it to exist. It was neither a government **de facto** nor **de jure**. That it was not in such possession of the Government property and agencies as entitled it to recognition is conclusively proved by a note found in the files of the legation at Honolulu, addressed by the declared head of the Provisional Government to Minister Stevens, dated January 17, 1893, in which he acknowledges with expressions of appreciation the minister's recognition of the Provisional Government, and states that it is not yet in the possession of the station house (the place where a large number of the Queen's troops were quartered), though the same had been demanded of the Queen's officers in charge. Nevertheless, this wrongful recognition by our minister placed the Government of the Queen in a position of most perilous perplexity. On the one hand she had possession of the palace, of the barracks, and of the police station, and had at her command at least 500 fully armed men and several pieces of artillery. Indeed, the whole military force of her Kingdom was on her side and at her disposal, while the committee of safety, by actual search, had discovered that there were but very few arms in Honolulu that were not in the service of the Government.

In this state of things, if the Queen could have dealt with the insurgents alone, her course would have been plain and the result unmistakable. But the United States had allied itself with her enemies, had recognized them as the true Government of Hawaii, and had put her and her adherents in the position of opposition against lawful authority. She knew that she could not withstand the power of the United States, but she believed that she might safely trust to its justice. Accordingly, some hours after the recognition of the Provisional Government by the United States minister, the palace, the barracks, and the police station, with all the military resources of the country, were delivered up by the Queen upon the representation made to her that her cause would thereafter be reviewed at Washington, and while protesting that she surrendered to the superior force of the United States, whose minister had caused United States troops to be landed at Honolulu and declared that he would support the Provisional Government, and that she yielded her authority to prevent collision of armed forces and loss of life, and only until such time as the United States, upon the facts being presented to it, should undo the action of its representative and reinstate her in the authority she claimed as the constitutional sovereign of the Hawaiian Islands.

This protest was delivered to the chief of the Provisional Government, who indorsed thereon his acknowledgment of its receipt. The terms of the protest were read without dissent by those assuming to constitute the Provisional Government, who were certainly charged with the knowledge that the Queen, instead of finally abandoning her power, had appealed to the justice of the United States for reinstatement in her authority; and yet the Provisional Government, with this unanswered protest in its hand, hastened to negotiate with the United States for the permanent banishment of the Queen from power and for a sale of her Kingdom.

Our country was in danger of occupying the position of having actually set up a temporary government on foreign soil for the purpose of acquiring through that agency territory which we had wrongfully put in its possessions. The control of both sides of a bargain acquired in such a manner is called by a familiar and unpleasant name when found in private transactions. We are not without a precedent showing how scrupulously we avoided such accusations in former days. After the people of Texas had declared their independence of Mexico they resolved that on the acknowledgment of their independence by the United States they would seek admission into the Union. Several months after the battle of San Jacinto, by which Texan independence was practically assured and established, President Jackson declined to recognize it, alleging as one of his reasons that in the circumstances it became us "to beware of a too early movement, as it might subject us, however unjustly, to the imputation of seeking to establish the claim of our neighbors to a territory with a view to its subsequent acquisition by ourselves." This is in marked contrast with the hasty recognition of a government openly and concededly set up for the purpose of tendering to us territorial annexation.

I believe that a candid and thorough examination of the facts will force the conviction that the Provisional Government owes its existence to an armed invasion by the United States. Fair-minded people, with the evidence before them, will hardly claim that the Hawaiian Government was overthrown by the people of the islands or that the Provisional Government had ever existed with their consent. I do not understand that any member of this Government claims that the people would uphold it by their suffrages if they were allowed to vote on the question.

While naturally sympathizing with every effort to establish a republican form of government, it has been the settled policy of the United States to concede to people of foreign countries the same freedom and independence in the management of their domestic affairs that we have always claimed for ourselves, and it has been our practice to recognize revolutionary governments as soon as it became apparent that they were supported by the people. For illustration of this rule I need only to refer to the revolution in Brazil in 1889, when our minister was instructed to recognize the Republic "so soon as a majority of the people of Brazil should have signified their assent to its establishment and maintenance," to the revolution in Chile in 1891, when our minister was directed to recognize the new Government "if it was accepted by the people," and to the revolution in Venezuela in 1892, when our recognition was accorded on condition that the new Government was "fully established, in possession of the power of the nation, and accepted by the people."

As I apprehend the situation, we are brought face to face with the following conditions:

The lawful Government of Hawaii was overthrown without the drawing of a sword or the firing of a shot by a process every step of which, it may safely be asserted, is directly traceable to and dependent for its success upon the agency of the United States acting through its diplomatic and naval representatives.

But for the notorious predilections of the United States minister for annexation the committee of safety, which should be called the committee of annexation, would never have existed.

But for the landing of the United States forces upon false pretexts respecting the danger to life and property the committee would never have exposed themselves to the pains and penalties of treason by undertaking the subversion of the Queen's Government.

But for the presence of the United States forces in the immediate vicinity and in position to afford all needed protection and support the committee would not have proclaimed the Provisional Government from the steps of the Government building.

And finally, but for the lawless occupation of Honolulu under false pretexts by the United States forces, and but for Minister Steven's recognition of the Provisional Government when the United States forces were its sole support and constituted its only military strength, the Queen and her Government would never have yielded to the Provisional Government, even for a time and for the sole purpose of submitting her case to the enlightened justice of the United States.

Believing, therefore, that the United States could not, under the circumstances disclosed, annex the islands without justly incurring the imputation of acquiring them by unjustifiable methods, I shall not again submit the treaty of annexation to the Senate for its consideration, and in the instructions to Minister Willis, a copy of which accompanies this message, I have directed him to so inform the Provisional Government.

But in the present instance our duty does not, in my opinion, end with refusing to consummate this questionable transaction. It has been the boast of our Government that it seeks to do justice in all things without regard to the strength or weakness of those with whom it deals. I mistake the American people if they favor the odious doctrine that there is no such thing as international morality; that there is one law for a strong nation and another for a weak one, and that even by indirection a strong power may with impunity despoil a weak one of its territory.

By an act of war, committed with the participation of a diplomatic representative of the United States and without authority of Congress, the Government of a feeble but friendly and confiding people has been overthrown. A substantial wrong has thus been done which a due regard for our national character as well as the rights of the injured people requires we should endeavor to repair. The Provisional Government has not assumed a republican or other constitutional form, but has remained a mere executive council or oligarchy, set up without the assent of the people. It has not sought to find a permanent basis of popular support and has given no evidence of an intention to do so. Indeed, the representatives of that Government assert that the people of Hawaii are unfit for popular government and frankly avow that they can be best ruled by arbitrary or despotic power.

The law of nations is founded upon reason and justice, and the rules of conduct governing individual relations between citizens or subjects of a civilized state are equally applicable as between enlightened nations. The considerations that international law is without a court for its enforcement and that obedience to its commands practically depends upon good faith instead of upon the mandate of a superior tribunal only give additional sanction to the law itself and brand any deliberate infraction of it not merely as a wrong, but as a disgrace. A man of true honor protects the unwritten word which binds his conscience more scrupulously, if possible, than he does the bond a breach of which subjects him to legal liabilities, and the United States, in aiming to maintain itself as one of the most enlightened nations, would do its citizens gross injustice if it applied to its international relations any other than a high standard of honor and morality. On that ground the United States can not properly be put in the position of countenancing a wrong after its commission any more than in that of consenting to it in advance. On that ground it can not allow itself to refuse to redress an injury inflicted through an abuse of power by officers clothed with its authority and wearing its uniform; and on the same ground, if a feeble but friendly state is in danger of being robbed of its independence and its sovereignty by a misuse of the name and power of the United States, the United States can not fail to vindicate its honor and its sense of justice by an earnest effort to make all possible reparation.

These principles apply to the present case with irresistible force when the special conditions of the Queen's surrender of her sovereignty are recalled. She surrendered, not to the Provisional Government, but to the United States. She surrendered, not absolutely and permanently, but temporarily and conditionally until such time as the facts could be considered by the United States. Furthermore, the Provisional Government acquiesced in her surrender in that manner and on those terms, not only by tacit consent, but through the positive acts of some members of that Government, who urged her peaceable submission, not merely to avoid bloodshed, but because she could place implicit reliance upon the justice of the United States and that the whole subject would be finally considered at Washington.

I have not, however, overlooked an incident of this unfortunate affair which remains to be mentioned. The members of the Provisional Government and their supporters, though not entitled to extreme sympathy, have been led to their present predicament of revolt against the Government of the Queen by the indefensible encouragement and assistance of our diplomatic representative. This fact may entitle them to claim that in our effort to rectify the wrong committed some regard should be had for their safety. This sentiment is strongly seconded by my anxiety to do nothing which would invite either harsh retaliation on the part of the Queen or violence and bloodshed in any quarter. In the belief that the Queen, as well as her enemies, would be willing to adopt such a course as would meet these conditions, and in view of the fact that both the Queen and the Provisional Government had at one time apparently acquiesced in a reference of the entire case to the United States Government, and considering the further fact that in any event the Provisional Government by its own declared limitation was only "to exist until terms of union with the United States of America have been negotiated and agreed upon." I hoped that after the assurance to the members of that Government that such union could not be consummated I might compass a peaceful adjustment of the difficulty.

Actuated by these desires and purposes, and not unmindful of the inherent perplexities of the situation nor of the limitations upon my power, I instructed Minister Willis to advise the Queen and her supporters of my desire to aid in the restoration of the status existing before the lawless landing of the United States forces at Honolulu on the 16th of January last if such restoration could be effected upon terms providing for clemency as well as justice to all parties concerned. The conditions suggested, as the instructions show, contemplate a general amnesty to those concerned in setting up the Provisional Government and a recognition of all its **bona fide** acts and obligations. In short, they require that the past should be buried and that the restored Government should reassume its authority as if its continuity had not been interrupted. These conditions have not proved acceptable to the Queen, and though she has been informed that they will be insisted upon and that unless acceded to the efforts of the President to aid in the restoration of her Government will cease, I have not thus far learned that she is willing to yield them her acquiescence. The check which my plans have thus encountered has prevented their presentation to the members of the Provisional Government, while unfortunate public misrepresentations of the situation and exaggerated statements of the sentiments of our people have obviously injured the prospects of successful Executive mediation.

I therefore submit this communication, with its accompanying exhibits, embracing Mr. Blount's report, the evidence and statements taken by him at Honolulu, the instructions given to both Mr. Blount and Minister Willis, and correspondence connected with the affair in hand.

In commending this subject to the extended powers and wide discretion of the Congress I desire to add the assurance that I shall be much gratified to cooperate in any legislative plan which may be devised for the solution of the problem before us which is consistent with American honor, integrity, and morality.

GROVER CLEVELAND

VETO OF SILVER BULLION COINAGE BILL
March 29, 1894

The Bland bill for coining silver seigniorage and other loose bullion in the Treasury created a serious problem among the sound money advocates. Seigniorage represents the gain which the government acquires when it has purchased bullion at a price less than the value stamped on the metal when coined. Enough metal was accumulated in the Treasury to coin about $55,150,000 in silver dollars. Cleveland was almost tempted to yield to expediency and sign the bill, but he recognized the serious threat to the financial condition of the nation. He vetoed the bill, indicating that its enactment would be a step backward from the sound financial intentions which had been announced by the repeal of the Sherman Silver Purchase Act and would have checked the financial recovery which had been slowly getting underway.

Executive Mansion, March 29, 1894

To the House of Representatives:

I return without my approval House bill No. 4956 entitled "An act directing the coinage of the silver bullion held in the Treasury, and for other purposes."

My strong desire to avoid disagreement with those in both Houses of Congress who have supported this bill would lead me to approve it if I could believe that the public good would not be thereby endangered and that such action on my part would be a proper discharge of official duty. Inasmuch, however, as I am unable to satisfy myself that the proposed legislation is either wise or opportune, my conception of the obligations and responsibilities attached to the great office I hold forbids the indulgence of my personal desire and inexorably confines me to that course which is dictated by my reason and judgment and pointed out by a sincere purpose to protect and promote the general interests of our people.

The financial disturbance which swept over the country during the last year was unparalleled in its severity and disastrous consequences. There seemed to be almost an entire displacement of faith in our financial ability and a loss of confidence in our fiscal policy. Among those who attempted to assign causes for our distress it was very generally conceded that the operation of a provision of law then in force which required the Government to purchase monthly a large amount of silver bullion and issue its notes in payment therefor was either entirely or to a large extent responsible for our condition. This led to the repeal on the 1st day of November, 1893, of this statutory provision.

We had, however, fallen so low in the depths of depression and timidity and apprehension had so completely gained control in financial circles that our rapid recuperation could not be reasonable expected. Our recovery has, nevertheless, steadily progressed, and though less than five months have elapsed since the repeal of the mischevious silver-purchase requirement a wholesome improvement is unmistakably apparent. Confidence in our absolute solvency is to such an extent reinstated and faith in our disposition to adhere to sound financial methods is so far restored as to produce the most encouraging results both at home and abroad. The wheels of domestic industry have been slowly set in motion and the tide of foreign investment has again started in our direction.

Our recovery being so well under way, nothing should be done to check our convalescence; nor should we forget that a relapse at this time would almost surely reduce us to a lower stage of financial distress than that from which we are just emerging.

I believe that if the bill under consideration would become a law, it would be regarded as a retrogression from the financial intentions indicated by our recent repeal of the provision forcing silver-bullion purchases; that it would weaken, if it did not destroy, returning faith and confidence on our sound financial tendencies, and that as a consequence our progress to renewed business health would be unfortunately checked and a return to our recent distressing plight seriously threatened.

This proposed legislation is so related to the currency conditions growing out of the law compelling the purchase of silver by the Government that a glance at such conditions and a partial review of the law referred to may not be unprofitable.

Between the 14th day of August, 1890, when the law became operative, and the 1st day of November, 1893, when the clause it contained directing the purchase of silver was repealed, there were purchased by the Secretary of the Treasury more than 168,000,000 ounces of silver bullion. In payment for this bullion the Government issued its Treasury notes, of various denominations, amounting to nearly $156,000,000, which notes were immediately added to the currency in circulation among our people. Such notes were by the law made legal tender in payment of all debts, public and private, except when otherwise expressly stipulated, and were made receivable for customs, taxes, and all public dues, and when so received might be reissued. They were also permitted to be held by banking associations as a part of their lawful reserves.

On the demand of the holders these Treasury notes were to be redeemed in gold or silver coin, in the discretion of the Secretary of the Treasury; but it was declared as a part of this redemption provision that it was "the established policy of the United States to maintain the two metals on a parity with each other upon the present legal ratio or such ratio as may be provided by law." The money coined from such bullion was to be standard silver dollars, and after directing the immediate coinage of a little less than 28,000,000 ounces the law provided that as much of the remaining bullion should be thereafter coined as might be necessary to provide for the redemption of the Treasury notes issued on its purchase, and that "any gain or seigniorage arising from such coinage shall be accounted for and paid into the Treasury."

This gain or seigniorage evidently indicates so much of the bullion owned by the Government as should remain after using a sufficient amount to coin as many standard silver dollars as should equal in number the dollars represented by the Treasury notes issued in payment of the entire quantity of bullion. These Treasury notes now outstanding and in circulation amount to $152,951,280, and although there has been thus far but a comparatively small amount of this bullion coined, yet the so-called gain or seigniorage, as above defined, which would arise from the coinage of the entire mass has been easily ascertained to be a quantity of bullion sufficient to make when coined 55,156,681 standard silver dollars.

Considering the present intrinsic relation between gold and silver, the maintenance of the parity between the two metals, as mentioned in this law, can mean nothing less than the maintenance of such a parity in the estimation and confidence of the people who use our money in their daily transactions. Manifestly the maintenance of this parity can only be accomplished, so far as it is affected by these Treasury notes and in the estimation of the holders of the same, by giving to such holders on their redemption to the discretion of the Secretary of the Treasury, the exercise of this discretion, if opposed to the demands of the holder, is entirely inconsistent with the effective and beneficial maintenance of the parity between the two metals.

If both gold and silver are to serve us as money and if they together are to supply to our people a safe and stable currency, the necessity of preserving this parity is obvious. Such necessity has been repeatedly conceded in the platforms of both political parties and in our Federal statutes. It is nowhere more emphatically recognized than in the recent law which repealed the provision under which the bullion now on hand was purchased. This law insists upon the "maintenance of the parity in value of the coins of the two metals and the equal power of every dollar at all times in the markets and in the payment of debts."

The Secretary of the Treasury has therefore, for the best of reasons, not only promptly complied with every demand for the redemption of these Treasury notes in gold, but the present situation as well as the letter and spirit of the law appear plainly to justify, if they do not enjoin upon him, a continuation of such redemption.

The conditions I have endeavored to present may be thus summarized:

First. The Government has purchased and now has on hand sufficient silver bullion to permit the coinage of all the silver dollars necessary to redeem in such dollars the Treasury notes issued for the purchase of said silver bullion, and enough besides to coin, as gain or seigniorage, 55,156,681 additional standard silver dollars.

Second. There are outstanding and now in circulation Treasury notes issued in payment of the bullion purchased amounting to $152,951,280. These notes are legal tender in payment of all debts, public and private, except when otherwise expressly stipulated; they are receivable for customs, taxes, and all public dues; when held by banking associations they may be counted as part of their lawful reserves, and they are redeemed by the Government in gold at the option of the holder. These advantageous attributes were deliberately attached to these notes at the time of their issue. They are fully understood by our people to whom such notes have been distributed as currency, and have inspired confidence in their safety and value, and have undoubtedly thus induced their continued and contented use as money, instead of anxiety for their redemption. . . .

We have now outstanding more than $338,000,000 in silver certificates issued under existing laws. They are serving the purpose of money usefully and without question. Our gold reserve, amounting to only a little more than $100,000,000 is directly charged with the redemption of $346,000,000 of United States notes. When it is proposed to inflate our silver currency it is a time for strengthening our gold reserve instead of depleting it. I can not conceive of a longer step toward silver monometallism than we take when we spend our gold to buy silver certificates for circulation, especially in view of the practical difficulties surrounding the replenishment of our gold.

This leads me to earnestly present the desirability of granting to the Secretary of the Treasury a better power than now exists to issue bonds to protect our gold reserve when for any reason it should be necessary. Our currency is in such a confused condition and our financial affairs are apt to assume at any time so critical a position that it seems to me such a course is dictated by ordinary prudence.

I am not insensible to the arguments in favor of coining the bullion seigniorage now in the Treasury, and I believe it could be done safely and with advantage if the Secretary of the Treasury had the power to issue bonds at a low rate of interest under authority in substitution of that now existing and better suited to the protection of the Treasury.

I hope a way will present itself in the near future for the adjustment of our monetary affairs in such a comprehensive and conservative manner as will accord to silver its proper place in our currency; but in the meantime I am extremely solicitous that whatever action we take on this subject may be such as to prevent loss and discouragement to our people at home and the destruction of confidence in our financial management abroad.

GROVER CLEVELAND

PROCLAMATION:
Martial Law In Chicago
July 8, 1894

As a result of the violence connected with the Pullman Strike in Chicago, Illinois, President Cleveland was urged by Attorney General Richard Olney to send troops into the city to restore order. He proceeded to act contrary to the wishes of Governor John Altgeld of Illinois. Cleveland was applauded by the business community for his action at the time, but the incident was to be remembered with obvious distaste by labor.

Whereas, by reason of unlawful obstructions, combinations, and assemblages of persons, it has become impracticable, in the judgment of the President, to enforce by the ordinary course of judicial proceedings the laws of the United States within the State of Illinois, and especially in the city of Chicago within said State; and

Whereas, for the purpose of enforcing the faithful execution of the laws of the United States and protecting its property and removing obstructions to the United States mails in the State and city aforesaid, the President has employed a part of the military forces of the United States:

Now, therefore, I, Grover Cleveland, President of the United States, do hereby admonish all good citizens and all persons who may be or may come within the city and State aforesaid against aiding, countenancing, encouraging, or taking any part in such unlawful obstruction, combinations, and assemblages; and I hereby warn all persons engaged in or in any way connected with such unlawful obstructions, combinations, and assemblages to disperse and retire peaceably to their respective adobes on or before 12 o'clock noon on the 9th day of July instant.

Those who disregard this warning and persist in taking part with a riotous mob in forcibly resisting and obstructing the execution of the laws of the United States or interfering with the functions of the Government or destroying or attempting to destroy the property belonging to the United States or under its protection can not be regarded otherwise than as public enemies.

Troops employed against such a riotous mob will act with all the moderation and forbearance consistent with the accomplishment of the desired end, but the stern necessities that confront them will not with certainty permit discrimination between guilty participants and those who are mingled with them from curiosity and without criminal intent. The only safe course, therefore, for those not actually unlawfully participating is to abide at their homes, or at least not to be found in the neighborhood of riotous assemblages.

While there will be no hesitation or vacillation in the decisive treatment of the guilty, this warning is especially intended to protect and save the innocent.

In testimony whereof I have hereunto set my hand and caused the seal of the United States to be hereto affixed.

Done at the city of Washington, this 8th day of July, A.D. 1894, and of the Independence of the United States the one hundred and nineteenth.

GROVER CLEVELAND

SPECIAL MESSAGE TO CONGRESS:
Currency Issue
January 28, 1895

President Cleveland indicated the growing lack of confidence in the Government's ability to pay its obligations in gold. The two problems connected with the crisis were the issuance of the wrong type of bonds which allows for payment in coin as well as gold and the requirement that all currency notes presented for redemption in gold had to be reissued. In order that the gold reserve be replenished Cleveland urged that the Secretary of the Treasury be authorized to issue a new type of bonds and also that he be permitted to redeem and cancel the United States legal-tender notes and Treasury Notes issued to purchase silver under the Sherman Silver Purchase Act.

EXECUTIVE MANSION, **January 28, 1895**

To the Senate and House of Representatives:

In my last annual message I commended to the serious consideration of the Congress the condition of our national finances, and in connection with the subject indorsed a plan of currency legislation which at that time seemed to furnish protection against impending danger. This plan has not been approved by the Congress. In the meantime the situation has so changed and the emergency now appears so threatening that I deem it my duty to ask at the hands of the legislative branch of the Government such prompt and effective action as will restore confidence in our financial soundness and avert business disaster and universal distress among our people.

Whatever may be the merits of the plan outlined in my annual message as a remedy for ills then existing and as a safeguard against the depletion of the gold reserve then in the Treasury, I am now convinced that its reception by the Congress and our present advanced stage of financial perplexity necessitate additional or different legislation.

With natural resources unlimited in variety and productive strength and with a people whose activity and enterprise seek only a fair opportunity to achieve national success and greatness, our progress should not be checked by a false financial policy and a heedless disregard of sound monetary laws, nor should the timidity and fear which they engender stand in the way of our prosperity.

It is hardly disputed that this predicament confronts us to-day. Therefore no one in any degree responsible for the making and execution of our laws should fail to see a patriotic duty in honestly and sincerely attempting to relieve the situation. Manifestly this effort will not succeed unless it is made untrammeled by the prejudice of partisanship and with a steadfast determination to resist the temptation to accomplish party advantage. We may well remember that if we are threatened with financial difficulties all our people in every station of life are concerned; and surely those who suffer will not receive the promotion of party interests as an excuse for permitting our present troubles to advance to a disastrous conclusion. It is also of the utmost importance that we approach the study of the problems presented as free as possible from the tyranny of preconceived opinions, to the end that in a common danger we may be able to seek with unclouded vision a safe and reasonable protection.

The real trouble which confronts us consists in a lack of confidence, widespread and constantly increasing, in the continuing ability or disposition of the Government to pay its obligations in gold. This lack of confidence grows to some extent out of the palpable and apparent embarrassment attending the efforts of the Government under existing laws to procure gold and to a greater extent out of the impossibility of either keeping it in the Treasury or canceling obligations by its expenditure after it is obtained.

The only way left open to the Government for procuring gold is by the issue and sale of its bonds. The only bonds that can be so issued were authorized nearly twenty-five years ago and are not well calculated to meet our present needs. Among other disadvantages, they are made payable in coin instead of specifically in gold, which in existing conditions detracts largely and in an increasing ratio from their desirability as investments. It is by no means certain that bonds of this description can much longer be disposed of at a price creditable to the financial character of our Government.

The most dangerous and irritating feature of the situation, however, remains to be mentioned. It is found in the means by which the Treasury is despoiled of the gold thus obtained without canceling a single Government obligation and solely for the benefit of those who find profit in shipping it abroad or whose fears induce them to hoard it at home. We have outstanding about five hundred millions of currency notes of the Government for which gold may be demanded, and, curiously enough, the law requires that when presented and, in fact, redeemed and paid in gold they shall be reissued. Thus the same notes may do duty many times in drawing gold from the Treasury; nor can the process be arrested as long as private parties, for profit or otherwise, see an advantage in repeating the operation. More than $300,000,000 in these notes have already been redeemed in gold, and notwithstanding such redemption they are all still outstanding.

Since the 17th day of January, 1894, our bonded interest-bearing debt has been increased $100,000,000 for the purpose of obtaining gold to replenish our coin reserve. Two issues were made amounting to fifty millions each, one in January and the other in November. As a result of the first issue there was realized something more than $58,000,000 in gold. Between that issue and the succeeding one in November, comprising a period of about ten months, nearly $103,000,000 in gold were drawn from the Treasury. This made the second issue necessary, and upon that more than fifty-eight millions in gold was again realized. Between the date of this second issue and the present time, covering a period of only about two months, more than $69,000,000 in gold have been drawn from the Treasury. These large sums of gold were expended without any cancellation of Government obligations or in any permanent way benefiting our people or improving our pecuniary situation.

The financial events of the past year suggest facts and conditions which should certainly arrest attention.

More than $172,000,000 in gold have been drawn out of the Treasury during the year for the purpose of shipment abroad or hoarding at home.

While nearly $103,000,000 of this amount was drawn out during the first ten months of the year, a sum aggregating more than two-thirds of that amount, being about $69,000,000, was drawn out during the following two months, thus indicating a marked acceleration of the depleting process with the lapse of time.

The obligations upon which this gold has been drawn from the Treasury are still outstanding and are available for use in repeating the exhausting operation with shorter intervals as our perplexities accumulate.

Conditions are certainly supervening tending to make the bonds which may be issued to replenish our gold less useful for that purpose.

An adequate gold reserve is in all circumstances absolutely essential to the upholding of our public credit and to the maintenance of our high national character.

Our gold reserve has again reached such a stage of diminution as to require its speedy reenforcement.

The aggravations that must inevitably follow present conditions and methods will certainly lead to misfortune and loss, not only to our national credit and prosperity and to financial enterprise, but to those of our people who seek employment as a means of livelihood and to those whose only capital is their daily labor.

It will hardly do to say that a simple increase of revenue will cure our troubles. The apprehension now existing and constantly increasing as to our financial ability does not rest upon a calculation of our revenue. The time has passed when the eyes of investors abroad and our people at home were fixed upon the revenues of the Government. Changed conditions have attracted their attention to the gold of the Government. There need be no fear that we can not pay our current expenses with such money as we have. There is now in the Treasury a comforable surplus of more than $63,000,000, but it is not in gold, and therefore does not meet our difficulty.

I can not see that differences of opinion concerning the extent to which silver ought to be coined or used in our currency should interfere with the counsels of those whose duty it is to rectify evils now apparent in our financial situation. They have to consider the question of national credit and the consequences that will follow from its collapse. Whatever ideas may be insisted upon as to silver or bimetallism, a proper solution of the question now pressing upon us only requires a recognition of gold as well as silver and a concession of its importance, rightfully or wrongfully acquired, as a basis of national credit, a necessity in the honorable discharge of our obligations payable in gold, and a badge of solvency. I do not understand that the real friends of silver desire a condition that might follow inaction or neglect to appreciate the meaning of the present exigency if it should result in the entire banishment of gold from our financial and currency arrangements.

Besides the Treasury notes, which certainly should be paid in gold, amounting to nearly $500,000,000, there will fall due in 1904 one hundred millions of bonds issued during the last year, for which we have received gold, and in 1907 nearly six hundred millions of 4 per cent bonds issued in 1877. Shall the payment of these obligations in gold be repudiated? If they are to be paid in such a manner as the preservation of our national honor and national solvency demands, we should not destroy or even imperil our ability to supply ourselves with gold for that purpose.

While I am not unfriendly to silver and while I desire to see it recognized to such an extent as is consistent with financial safety and the preservation of national honor and credit, I am not willing to see gold entirely banished from our currency and finances. To avert such a consequence I believe thorough and radical remedial legislation should be promptly passed. I therefore beg the Congress to give the subject immediate attention.

In my opinion the Secretary of the Treasury should be authorized to issue bonds of the Government for the purpose of procuring and maintaining a sufficient gold reserve and the redemption and cancellation of the United States legal-tender notes and the Treasury notes issued for the purchase of silver under the law of July 14, 1890. We should be relieved from the humiliating process of issuing bonds to procure gold to be immediately and repeatedly drawn out on these obligations for purposes not related to the benefit of our Government or our people. The principal and interest of these bonds should be payable on their face in gold, because they should be sold only for gold or its representative, and because there would now probably be difficulty in favorably disposing of bonds not containing this stipulation. I suggest that the bonds be issued in denominations of twenty and fifty dollars and their multiples and that they bear interest at a rate not exceeding 3 per cent per annum. I do not see why they should not be payable fifty years from their date. We of the present generation have large amounts to pay if we meet our obligations, and long bonds are most salable. The Secretary of the Treasury might well be permitted at his discretion to receive on the sale of bonds the legal-tender and Treasury notes to be retired, and of course when they are thus retired or redeemed in gold they should be canceled.

These bonds under existing laws could be deposited by national banks as security for circulation, and such banks should be allowed to issue circulation up to the face value of these or any other bonds so deposited, except bonds outstanding bearing only 2 per cent interest and which sell in the market at less than par. National banks should not be allowed to take out circulating notes of a less denomination than $10, and when such as are now outstanding reach the Treasury, except for redemption and retirement, they should be canceled and notes of the denomination of $10 and upward issued in their stead. Silver certificates of the denomination of $10 and upward should be replaced by certificates of the denominations under $10.

As a constant means for the maintenance of a reasonable supply of gold in the Treasury, our duties on imports should be paid in gold, allowing all other dues to the Government to be paid in any other form of money.

I believe all the provisions I have suggested should be embodied in our laws if we are to enjoy a complete reinstatement of a sound financial condition. They need not interfere with any currency scheme providing for the increase of the circulating medium through the agency of national or State banks that may commend itself to the Congress, since they can easily be adjusted to such a scheme. Objection has been made to the issuance of interest-bearing obligations for the purpose of retiring the noninterest-bearing legal-tender notes. In point of fact, however, these notes have burdened us with a large load of interest, and it is still accumulating. The aggregate interest on the original issue of bonds, the proceeds of which in gold constituted the reserve for the payment of these notes, amounted to $70,326,250 on January 1, 1895, and the annual charge for interest on these bonds and those issued for the same purpose during the last year will be $9,145,000, dating from January 1, 1895.

While the cancellation of these notes would not relieve us from the obligations already incurred on their account, these figures are given by way of suggesting that their existence has not been free from interest charges and that the longer they are oustanding, judging from the experience of the last year, the more expensive they will become.

In conclusion I desire to frankly confess my reluctance to issuing more bonds in present circumstances and with no better results than have lately followed that course. I can not, however, refrain from adding to an assurance of my anxiety to cooperate with the present Congress in any reasonable measure of relief an expression of my determination to leave nothing undone which furnishes a hope for improving the situation or checking a suspicion of our disinclination or disability to meet with the strictest honor every national obligation.

GROVER CLEVELAND

SPECIAL MESSAGE TO CONGRESS:
Venezuelan Boundary Dispute
December 17, 1895

President Cleveland had been determined for quite a long period of time to urge a final settlement of the Venezuelan Boundary dispute. He maintained that the British were wrong in their insistence that the Monroe Doctrine did not apply in this case. He believed that the dispute had reached a stage in which the United States had to take part. Consequently, he requested that Congress appropriate money to cover the expenses of a commission to investigate and report on the true boundary line.

Executive Mansion, December 17, 1895

To the Congress:

In my annual message addressed to the Congress on the 3d instant I called attention to the pending boundary controversy between Great Britain and the Republic of Venezuela and recited the substance of a representation made by this government to Her Britannic Majesty's Government suggesting reasons why such dispute should be submitted to arbitration for settlement and inquiring whether it would be so submitted.

The answer of the British Government, which was then awaited, has since been received, and, together with the dispatch to which it is a reply, is hereto appended.

Such reply is embodied in two communications addressed by the British prime minister to Sir Julian Pauncefote, the British ambassador at this capital. It will be seen that one of these communications is devoted exclusively to observations upon the Monroe Doctrine, and claims that in the present instance a new and strange extension and development of this doctrine is insisted on by the United States; that the reasons justifying an appeal to the doctrine enunciated by President Monroe are generally inapplicable "to the state of things in which we live at the present day," and especially inapplicable to a controversy involving the boundary between Great Britain and Venezuela.

Without attempting extended argument in reply to these positions, it may not be amiss to suggest that the doctrine upon which we stand is strong and sound, because its enforcement is important to our peace and safety as a nation and is essential to the integrity of our free institutions and the tranquil maintenance of our distinctive form of government. It was intended to apply to every stage of our national life and can not become obsolete while our Republic endures. If the balance of power is justly a cause for jealous anxiety among the Governments of the Old World and a subject for our absolute noninterference, none the less is an observance of the Monroe doctrine of vital concern to our people and their Government.

Assuming, therefore, that we may properly insist upon this doctrine without regard to "the state of things in which we live" or any changed conditions here or elsewhere, it is not apparent why its application may not be invoked in the present controversy.

If a European power by an extension of its boundaries takes possession of the territory of one of our neighboring Republics against its will and in derogation of its rights, it is difficult to see why to that extent such European power does not thereby attempt to extend its system of government to that portion of this continent which is thus taken. This is the precise action which President Monroe declared to be "dangerous to our peace and safety," and it can make no difference whether the European system is extended by an advance of frontier or otherwise.

It is also suggested in the British reply that we should seek to apply the Monroe doctrine to the pending dispute because it does not embody any principle of international law which "is founded on the general consent of nations," and that "no statesman, however eminent, and no nation, however powerful, are competent to insert into the code of international law a novel principle which was never recognized before and which has not since been accepted by the government of any other country."

Practically the principle for which we contend has peculiar, if not exclusive, relation to the United States. It may not have been admitted in so many words to the code of international law, but since in international councils every nation is entitled to the rights belonging to it, if the enforcement of the Monroe doctrine is something we may justly claim it has its place in the code of international law as certainly and as securely as if it were specifically mentioned; and when the United States is a suitor before the high tribunal that administers international law the question to be determined is whether or not we present claims which the justice of that code of law can find to be right and valid.

The Monroe doctrine finds its recognition in those principles of international law which are based upon the theory that every nation shall have its rights protected and its just claims enforced.

Of course this Government is entirely confident that under the sanction of this doctrine we have clear rights and undoubted claims. Nor is this ignored in the British reply. The prime minister, while not admitting that the Monroe doctrine is applicable to present conditions, states:

In declaring that the United States would resist any such enterprise if it was contemplated, President Monroe adopted a policy which received the entire sympathy of the English Government of that date.

He further declares:

Though the language of President Monroe is directed to the attainment of objects which most Englishmen would agree to be salutary, it is impossible to admit that they have been inscribed by any adequate authority in the code of international law.

Again he says:

They (Her Majesty's Government) fully concur with the view which President Monroe apparently entertained, that any disturbance of the existing territorial distribution in that hemisphere by any fresh acquisitions on the part of any European State would be a highly inexpedient change.

In the belief that the doctrine for which we contend was clear and definite, that it was founded upon substantial considerations and involved our safety and welfare, that it was fully applicable to our present conditions and to the state of the world's progress, and that it was directly related to the pending controversy, and without any conviction as to the final merits of the dispute, but anxious to learn in a satisfactory and conclusive manner whether Great Britain sought under a claim of boundary to extend her possessions on this continent without right, or whether she merely sought possession of territory fairly included within her lines of ownership, this Government proposed to the Government of Great Britain to resort to arbitration as the proper means of settling the question, to the end that a vexatious boundary dispute between the two contestants might be determined and our exact standing and relation in respect to the controversy might be made clear.

It will be seen from the correspondence herewith submitted that this proposition has been declined by the British Government upon ground which in the circumstances seem to me to be far from satisfactory. It is deeply disappointing that such an appeal, actuated by the most friendly feelings toward both nations directly concerned, addressed to the sense of justice and to the magnanimity of one of the great powers of the world, and touching its relations to one comparatively weak and small, should have produced no better results.

The course to be pursued by this Government in view of the present condition does not appear to admit of serious doubt. Having labored fruitfully for many years to induce Great Britain to submit this dispute to impartial arbitration, and having been now finally apprised of her refusal to do so, nothing remains but to accept the situation, to recognize its plain requirements, and deal with it accordingly. Great Britain's present proposition has never thus far been regarded as admissible by Venezuela, though any adjustment of the boundary which that country may deem for her advantage and may enter into of her own free will can not of course be objected to by the United States.

Assuming, however, that the attitude of Venezuela will remain unchanged, the dispute has reached such a stage as to make it now incumbent upon the United States to take measures to determine with sufficient certainty for its justification what is the true divisional line between the Republic of Venezuela and British Guiana. The inquiry to that end should of course be conducted carefully and judicially, and due weight should be given to all available evidence, records, and facts in support of the claims of both parties.

In order that such an examination should be prosecuted in a thorough and satisfactory manner, I suggest that the Congress make an adequate appropriation for the expenses of a commission, to be appointed by the Executive, who shall make the necessary investigation and report upon the matter with the least possible delay. When such report is made and accepted it will, in my opinion, be the duty of the United States to resist by every means in its power, as a willful aggression upon its rights and interests, the appropriation by Great Britain of any lands or the exercise of governmental jurisdiction over any territory which after investigation we have determined of right belongs to Venezuela.

In making these recommendations I am fully alive to the responsibility incurred and keenly realize all the consequences that may follow.

I am, nevertheless, firm in my conviction that while it is a grievous thing to contemplate the two great English-speaking peoples of the world as being otherwise then friendly competitors in the onward march of civilization and strenuous and worthy rivals in all the arts of peace, there is no calamity which a great nation can invite which equals that which follows a supine submission to wrong and injustice and the consequent loss of national self-respect and honor, beneath which are shielded and defended a people's safety and greatness.

GROVER CLEVELAND

BIBLIOGRAPHICAL AIDS

The emphasis in this and subsequent volumes in the **Presidential Chronologies** series will be on the administrations of the presidents. The more important works on other aspects of their lives, either before or after their terms in office, are included since they may contribute to an understanding of the presidential careers.

The following bibliography is critically selected. Additional titles may be found in the Nevins biography of Cleveland (See biographies below) and in the standard guide. The student might also wish to consult **Reader's Guide to Periodical Literature** and **Social Sciences and Humanities Index** (formerly **International Index**) for recent articles in scholarly journals.

Additional chronological information not included in this volume because it did not relate to the president may be found in the **Encyclopedia of American History,** edited by Richard B. Morris, revised edition (New York, 1965).

Asterisks after titles refer to books currently available in paperback editions.

SOURCE MATERIALS

The major part of the material written to and many letters by and the diaries of Grover Cleveland is in the Library of Congress. It has been printed on microfilm in 164 reels.

Nevins, Allan, ed. **Grover Cleveland. Letters, 1850-1908.** New York, 1933. A valuable selection indicating the man and his times.

Presidential Papers Microfilm: Grover Cleveland Papers. Washington, D.C., 1958.

BIOGRAPHIES

Gilder, Richard Watson. **Grover Cleveland: A Record of Friendship.** New York, 1910. This volume deals more with Cleveland the man.

Lynch, Denis Tilden. **Grover Cleveland, A Man Four-Square.** New York, 1932. This work is a sympathetic study of Cleveland. The author makes no attempt at philosophical interpretation of his material.

McElroy, Robert McNutt. **Grover Cleveland, The Man and the Statesman.** 2 vols. New York, 1933. These two volumes are the authorized biography of Grover Cleveland. A well-written comprehensive work presenting many letters to strengthen the narrative.

Merrill, Horace Samuel. **Bourbon Leader: Grover Cleveland and the Democratic Party.** Boston, 1957. A well-written short biography of this leader of the Democracy. It will serve quite well when Nevins' detailed biography is too long.

Nevins, Allan. **Grover Cleveland: A Study in Courage.** New York, 1932. The definitive biography of Cleveland. Nevins had at his disposal valuable material not formerly available. Well-documented work.

Parker, George F. **Recollections of Grover Cleveland.** New York, 1909. A reminiscental work presenting Cleveland the man.

ESSAYS

The essay on Cleveland by Horace Samuel Merrill in the **Encyclopedia Americana** and that by George Harmon Knowles in the **Encyclopedia Britannica** are much too brief on the First Term. Discussion of the Second Term is much more detailed. Merrill's article is much more comprehensive on the whole. Frederic Logan Paxson's article on Cleveland in the **Dictionary of American Biography** deals with the three election campaigns and the major economic and diplomatic issues of Cleveland's Second Term. Discussion of the first term is somewhat inadequate. Victor P. DeSantis' essay of Grover Cleveland in **America's Ten Greatest Presidents,** edited by Morton Borden, is a fine analysis of Cleveland's domestic policy. Walter La Feber has presented an excellent view of Cleveland's problems in connection with the Venezuelan boundary dispute in the following essays: "The American Business Community and Cleveland's Venezuelan Message," **Business History Review,** vol. 34 (1960), pp. 393-402, and "The Background of Cleveland's Venezuelan Policy: A Reinterpretation," **American Historical Review,** vol. 66 (1960-1961), pp. 947-967.

MONOGRAPHS AND SPECIAL AREAS

Barnes, James A. **John G. Carlisle: Political Statesman.** New York, 1931. A partisan but forcible defense of Carlisle, particularly in relation to the bond issue.

DeSantis, Vincent P. **Republicans Face the Southern Question, The New Departure Years, 1877-1897.** New York, 1959. A fine account of the attempts of Republican Presidents to cultivate support in the South for their party. Shows that the Republicans were certainly persistent regardless of their failure.

Knoles, George Harmon. **The Presidential Campaign and Election of 1892.** Palo Alto, Calif. 1942. A complete picture of the electoral campaign showing how all social and political movements including populism were involved.

Lambert, John R. **Arthur Pue Gorman.** New York, 1953. A good analysis of this important congressman who was involved in the tariff issue.

Pratt, Julius. **Expansionsts of 1898: The Acquisition of Hawaii and the Spanish Islands.** Blatimore, 1936. A careful and complete discussion of the entire period.

THE CLEVELAND ERA

Goldman, Eric. **Rendezvous with Destiny.** New York, 1952. A lively account of certain elements of liberal thought in the period 1877 to 1914.

Hollingsworth, T. Rogers. **The Whirligig of Politics: The Democracy of Cleveland and Bryan.** Chicago, 1963. An excellent analysis of the basic struggles and tensions in American society from 1896 to 1904, and how these two Democratic leaders handled them.

James, Henry. **Richard Olney and His Public Service.** Boston, 1923. An excellent, though old, source book for the second Cleveland administration dealing with those important activities in which Olney played a part.

Josephson, Matthew. **The Politicos, 1865-1896.** New York, 1938. In this companion volume to **The Robber Barons,** the author reviews the politics of the United States during the Reconstruction to the defeat of Bryan in 1896.

Merrill, Horace Samuel. **Bourbon Democracy of the Middle West, 1865-1896.** Boston, 1953. A fine analysis of the Middle West, and the part which Democratic leaders played with their counterparts in the East and in industry.

LaFeber, Walter. **The New Empire: An Interpretation of American Expansion, 1860-1898.** Ithaca, 1963. An excellent, well-documented work discussing American developments in this important area of national experience.

Perkins, Dexter. **The Monroe Doctrine, 1865-1907.** Baltimore, 1937. An excellent and inclusive study of American affairs in relation to its role in hemispheric affairs.

Sievers, Harry Joseph. **Benjamin Harrison.** 3 vols. Chicago, 1952-1961. An excellent and sympathetic study of President Harrison, indicating important aspects of his administration. The author also analyzes the various differences of the two major political parties in the 1880's and 1890's.

WORKS BY GROVER CLEVELAND

Good Citizenship. New York, 1908.

Independence of the Executive. 1900.

Presidential Problems. Princeton, 1904.

THE PRESIDENCY

Bailey, Thomas Andrew. **Presidential Greatness: The Image and the Man from George Washington to the Present.** New York, 1966. A good critical study of the qualities of presidential greatness, listing 43 methods for measuring presidential ability. Bailey differs from the "Near Great" ranking of Cleveland in the Schlesinger polls, rating him "no better than average."

Binkley, Wilfred E. **The Man in the White House: His Powers and His Duties,** rev. ed. New York, 1964. A fine historically-oriented survey of the Presidency in its various aspects.

Corwin, Edward Samuel. **The President: Office and Powers; History and Analysis of Practice and Opinions.** 4th ed. New York, 1957. A factual and well-documented older historical account of the position of the President.

Kane, Joseph Nathan. **Facts about the President.** New York, 1959. Detailed factual information about each president from Washington to Eisenhower, as well as comparative data and statistics concerning the individuals and the office of the position of the presidency.

Koenig, Louis W. **The Chief Executive.** New York, 1964. Historical discussion of presidential powers, comparing America's strong and weak presidents.

Laski, Harold J. **The American Presidency, An Interpretation.** New York, 1949. A classical study of the American executive by an Englishman.

Rossiter, Clinton Lawrence. **The American Presidency.** 2nd ed. New York, 1960. A fine discussion of the powers and limitations of the President.

Schlesinger, Arthur Meyer. "The United States Presidents," **Life Magazine,** XXV (November 1, 1948), 65 ff.

————. "Our Presidents: A Rating by 75 Historians," **New York Times Magazine,** July 29, 1962, 12 ff.

NAME INDEX

TITLES IN THE OCEANA

PRESIDENTIAL CHRONOLOGY SERIES

Senior Editor: Howard F. Bremer

Reference books containing Chronology - Documents - Bibliographical Aids for each President covered.

1. GEORGE WASHINGTON   96 pages/$3.00
       edited by Howard F. Bremer

2. JOHN ADAMS   96 pages/$3.00
       edited by Howard F. Bremer

3. JAMES BUCHANAN   96 pages/$3.00
       edited by Irving J. Sloan

4. GROVER CLEVELAND   128 pages/$4.00
       edited by Robert I. Vexler

5. FRANKLIN PIERCE   96 pages/$3.00
       edited by Irving J. Sloan

6. ULYSSES S. GRANT   128 pages/$4.00
       edited by Philip Moran

Books may be ordered from
OCEANA PUBLICATIONS, INC.
Dobbs Ferry, New York 10522

For Reference

Not to be taken from this room